Adventures in Eating II:

A Guide to Denver's Ethnic Markets, Bakeries and Gourmet Stores

BY
SUSAN PERMUT

©1996, Better Business Communications
Denver, Colorado

© 1996 by Better Business Communications

ALL RIGHTS RESERVED. No part of this book may be reproduced in any manner without the express permission of the publisher, except by a reviewer who may quote brief passages. This includes any kind of electronic copying, photocopying, recording or reproduction by any other means.

Printed in the United States of America

First Edition
ISBN 0-9638153-4-2

Cover design by Skip Koebbeman
Photography by Susan Permut
Book design by Skip Koebbeman
Questions, suggestions etc. may be addressed to:
Susan Permut, c/o Better Business Communications
957 S. Cole Drive, Lakewood CO 80228
Please contact us to sell this book to benefit your non-profit organization. We'd be happy to consider a special price for you.

Contents

Eating Adventures Continue–4

    I Bakeries–4
   II Delicatessens–42
  III Markets–71
  IV Chocolate–132
   V Ice Cream–140
  VI Coffee–144

Index–154

Eating Adventures Continue

Welcome to the feast! Continuing forays into the growing world of ethnic food in Denver has spawned a whole new edition of Adventures in Eating! In the past year or so, no less than four Polish delis, a Caribbean bakery, a Filipino market and restaurant, and numerous other purveyors of delectable edibles have opened. We've also added places in Boulder and outlying areas and come up with all new and exciting recipes for you to use with the ingredients you find.

We work hard to make sure the hours and days that places are open are accurate, but please call before you go. Changes in family circumstances, the season or the marketplace may cause unexpected changes in hours.

Many items are seasonal, and so even though they were available when I visited the stores, they might not be when you visit. I give a general idea of the kinds of things carried by each store, but hope you discover other products and ingredients for yourself. Also, in case you wonder about the many different spellings of the same word, I usually use the spelling used by each individual store, so you can find the ingredients more easily.

Thank you once more to all the shopkeepers, bakers, sausage makers, coffee brewers, chocolatiers and cake decorators who allowed me to explore their stores, their methods, their ideas and their lives. Special thanks to John Lehndorff of the Boulder Camera for his help in discovering Boulder coffee shops, and other Boulder places, to Jay Fox for introducing me to Gargaro's, to Kathy Strand for her Boulder bakery suggestions, and to many others for their helpful ideas. The pleasure of finding out about all the wonderful kinds of food we have available to us in the Denver metro area continues to grow. I hope you enjoy the adventure as much as I did!

Bread & Pastries

There isn't anything in the world much better than a loaf of crusty bread. Not only is it wonderful by itself, or simply slathered with olive oil or butter, but it makes any meal it's served with both more substantial and more elegant. We're fortunate that in Denver we have a wide variety of bakeries, so that we can find just about any kind of bread or pastry our hearts desire. There has been a resurgence of rustic breads recently, along with specialty breads topped or stuffed with delicious taste treats. Bagels have also increased in popularity. Bakeries are now more likely to serve lunch or deli foods as well as bread and pastries. Each bakery has its own specialties. Try them all!

American Bakeries

A Piece of Cake

Table Mesa Drive & Broadway, Boulder 499-5253
Monday–Friday, 7 am–6 pm. Saturday, 8 am–5 pm. Closed Sunday.

Poppy seed cake with raspberry filling is the specialty at this Boulder bakery. Scones range from currant to chocolate chip to coconut macadamia. Fruit sticks are apricot, raspberry, apple and strawberry cheese. Pies like strawberry rhubarb are popular, as are their special occasion cakes, often decorated with squiggles of icing confetti. Prices here are very reasonable, with cookies starting at only 30 cents.

Baker's Street

8181 E. Arapahoe Road, Englewood   770-1966
Monday–Thursday, 7 am–7 pm; Friday & Saturday, 7 am–8 pm.
Sunday, 8 am–5 pm.

There are more kinds of bread here than you can shake a baguette at. Multigrain, pugliese, country sourdough, jalapeño cheddar, green olive or raisin pecan sourdough–all baked fresh daily, beautifully displayed and looking as crusty and rustic as anything straight from the oven in a rural farmhouse. In contrast, the setting is bright and clean with tables scattered about and attractive display cases. Don't even try to resist, because you know you won't win. Just give in and try one of their scones (cream currant, oat or cranberry walnut), cinnamon swirls, brownie cakes or a jumbo sticky bun. Gourmet sandwiches and specialty coffees complete the yummy picture.

Bluepoint Bakery

1307 E. 6th Avenue   839-1820
Monday–Saturday, 7 am–7 pm. Closed Sunday.

Whether your weakness is breads or pastries, you could meet your waterloo at the Bluepoint. They have many different kinds of breads, from olive oil braids to lemon basil campagne. Pies and tortes are as beautiful to look at as to eat, including such delights as strawberry apricot pie and mocha torte. There are fruit-topped cheese tarts, florentines, which are almond cakes dipped in dark chocolate, lemon bars and fabulous citron tarts filled with lemon curd. Cookies include blackberry thumb prints, intriguing pistachio curry cookies and shortbread for only 40¢ a piece–up from 35¢, but still a steal! Breads and pastries at the Bluepoint are all delicious. Try everything at least once.

The Story of Pugliese Bread

There's a legend that anyone who wastes even crumbs of this rustic country bread will be condemned to Purgatory for as many years as they wasted crumbs   *– Baker's Street Gourmet Bakery*

Bobby Dazzler

4628 E. 23rd Avenue (23rd & Dexter) 320-4353
Monday–Friday, 7 am–7 pm; Saturday, 7 am–4 pm.
Closed Sunday.

Something really good or out of the ordinary is described in Australian slang as a "real bobby dazzler". Some of the breads and pastries at this small neighborhood bakery are exactly that! My favorite is their brioche with cream cheese and strawberries–it's fabulous. Their scones and other specialty breads are equally delicious. The bakery is run by Amy and Kate. Amy makes the cakes and pies, while Kate handles the breads. Their specialties are crusty, rustic breads, fresh fruit pies in season, custard pies, and cakes based on the traditional pound cake. They concentrate on specialty breads that can't be bought at the supermarket, like sourdough Italian and whole wheat Irish soda bread with rosemary, walnuts and garlic, one or two different rye breads a week, and their very popular bread sticks. Bobby Dazzler has always made their breads with natural sour starter, and uses European-style all-organic flours and other ingredients. The breads are baked on stones in the oven. Their Russian tea cakes and enormous pieces of carrot cake are not to be missed, and they have all the old favorite American cookies, like oatmeal raisin chocolate chip and coconut macaroons.

Bonjour Bakery

8172 S. Holly, Littleton 721-7547 Fax: 721-7617
Tuesday–Sunday, 6:30 am–7 pm. Closed Monday.

Chira Pongratananukul, formerly pastry chef at the Scanticon and also at the Glenmoor Country Club, runs this light and airy little suburban bakery. Her fresh fruit tarts sparkle in the case. An assortment of cheesecakes, including vanilla, amaretto and kahlua, vie for attention with napoleons, lemon tortes and chocolate mousse tortes. The gourmet bagels include one with a cheese topping, and muffins like apple walnut, cherry almond and blueberry cry out for a cappuccino or latte to accompany them. Breakfast and lunch are served here, and among the lunch offerings is an intriguing Indonesian salad of shredded cabbage topped with boiled potatoes, carrots, bean sprouts, cucumbers, hard-boiled egg and toasted onions, dressed with peanut sauce.

Child's Pastry Garden

Monaco & Yale 757-1285
Tuesday–Friday, 7 am–6:30 pm; Saturday, 8 am–6 pm;
Sunday, 10 am–3 pm; Monday, 8:30 am–6:30 pm.
Child's Pastry Shop
311 E. County Line, Littleton 347-0246
Tuesday–Saturday, 8 am–6 pm; Sunday, 10 am–3 pm;
Monday, 10 am–6 pm.

Child's specializes in special occasion cakes, for birthdays, weddings graduations and so on. In fact, their wedding cake brochure has a very interesting description of the wedding cake tradition. Perhaps the most romantic piece of folklore is the legend that promises an unmarried girl who sleeps with a piece of wedding cake under her pillow a dream about her future husband! Of course Child's is also a full-service bakery, with many different kinds of bread, dinner rolls, croissants and a large variety of pies and cakes. Many Denverites refuse to go anywhere else for their birthday cakes.

Daily Bread

1738 Pearl Street, Boulder 444-6549
Monday–Saturday, 6:30 am–9 pm. Sunday, 8 am–7 pm.

Daily Bread offers some wonderful hearth-baked breads baked in a stone-lined oven imported from France. Their crusty, rustic loaves are almost all baked using natural sourdough yeast starters rather than commercial baker's yeast. This process takes longer, but the taste buds tell you it's worth it. One of their most delightful breads is a sun dried tomato and fresh herb fougasse, a Provençal flat bread made with olive oil, sun dried tomatoes and rosemary. Other artisan breads include multigrain, Sicilian semolina, walnut bread, olive bread and a choice of city or country baguette. There's also a selection of sandwiches, muffins, cakes and cookies.

Evergreen Pastry Shop

3877 S. Colo. Hwy 74, Evergreen (Safeway Shopping Ctr) 674-2120
Monday–Friday, 6 am–6 pm; Saturday, 8 am–5 pm. Closed Sunday.

Paul Montgomery recently took over the Evergreen Pastry Shop, and is working to attract new customers and lure back old ones with semolina breads, specialty breads like apricot, raspberry and lemon, muffins like blueberry bran and date bran and an assortment of other treats, such as danish pastries, butter cookies, rugalach and cheesecakes. He's introducing specialty coffees, with coffee from the Scottish Roaster, a local coffee supplier, and offering the very best customer service he can. An interesting note: he recycles his breadcrumbs and bread that's "past its prime" by selling it as breadcrumbs to the local pizza parlor to sprinkle on their crust instead of corn meal.

Fratelli's

1200 E. Hampden, Englewood (Old Hampden at Downing) 761-4771
Monday–Thursday, 6:30 am–10:30 pm; Friday & Saturday till 11;
Sunday, 6:30 am–9 pm.

Fratelli's is an Italian restaurant and bakery. They make large quantities of fresh breadsticks every day, in several different flavors, all of them delicious. They have fresh danish, cinnamon rolls, caramel and pecan rolls, great homemade tortes, several varieties of fresh bread each day and daily special sweet breads and muffins.

At Christmas, Jim Plummer, owner of Fratelli's, makes panettone, a specialty from Siena in Italy. It's a dense, flat cake made with honey, almonds, citrus and candied citron, cocoa and spices. It's very rich and delicious, made with only just enough flour to hold all the fruits and nuts together. At Fratelli's, they also make their own fresh pasta for sale, as well. Fettucine and vermicelli are available every day. Ravioli, lasagne, and other Italian delights are also available in large quantities for parties.

Granny Scott's Pie Shop

3333 S. Wadsworth, #C-107 (Mission Trace Shopping Center) Lakewood 986-6240
Tuesday–Thursday, 7:30 am–7:30 pm; Friday, 7:30 am–9:30 pm; Saturday, 9:30 am–9:30 pm. Sunday, 9:30 am–3:30 pm.

The selection of pies varies daily, but some of the choices include Tennessee whiskey, Georgia peanut butter, chocolate pecan, Swiss chocolate cream, New England blueberry, Michigan cherry and caramel Granny Smith apple, all without processed fillings. As if this isn't enough, you can also find crusty breads like calamata olive and feta cheese, corn bread with bacon and green chiles or whole wheat and currant. Granny Smith's also offers light breakfasts, coffee, sandwiches and soup for lunch. If you're hungry for pies the way granny used to make them, try Granny Scott's.

Great Harvest Bread Company

765 S. Colorado Boulevard (Belcaro Shopping Center)   778-8877
Monday–Friday, 6 am–7 pm; Sunday, 6 am–6 pm.
Also: 80th & Wadsworth, Arvada   420-0500
South University & Orchard (Cherry Hills Marketplace)   347-8767
2525 Arapahoe, Boulder   442-3062

The sign on the door at the south store says, "No shirt? No shoes? No problem!" This typifies the wonderfully laid-back attitude at Great Harvest. All their bread is made from 100% organic wheat milled daily at each of their stores. Their breads include several kinds of whole wheat, as well as many specialty breads like oat poppy seed, date nut spice, jalapeño corn bread, orange pecan, tomato basil and many others. Not all specialty breads are always available, but they welcome orders. At the Belcaro store they're making a low-fat cinnamon roll, and all stores make low-fat muffins. The south store makes some unconventional breads on Tuesdays, including spelt bread, yeast-free and sugar-free breads. I just love walking in and being offered a slice of their bread to try. Great Harvest is great for good wholesome bread and a delightful outlook on life.

The Legend of the Wedding Cake

Even in ancient Rome, lovers celebrated the beginning of their lives together in a wedding ceremony. In those days it was the custom for the vestal virgins to bake a cake of salted meal which was broken above the bride's head to symbolize plenty, and eaten by the bride and groom a part of the marriage rite. Pieces of the cake were then carried by the bride to her new home and shared with relatives and friends. In time, the custom reached England, where a piece of cake was thought to bring good luck. Baskets of small, hard wafers were prepared for guests as souvenirs and were also given to the poor.

Finally, the wafers were replaced with a mound of small buns, over which the bride and groom kissed to symbolize prosperity and a long life. Eventually, a Frenchman added a sugar icing to hold the stack of buns together. Out of this tradition grew the lavish, many-tiered wedding cakes we know today.

From Dale & Sharon Goetz, A Piece of Cake
Used with permission.

Just From Scratch

4800 Baseline Road, Suite A-109, Boulder 494-3635
Tuesday–Saturday, 7 am–5 pm. Closed Sunday & Monday.

Jim and Linda Schuriche were traveling in Europe when Linda had the idea for this bakery. Since she's a pharmacist by trade with no formal training in baking, she taught herself to bake. For example, she developed a basic muffin recipe and now makes 25 different muffins from that one mixture, instead of making several different recipes. Breads include French, cinnamon white and wheat, and they make brioches daily. Scones are varied: currant, almond, blueberry, cranberry or peach walnut. Their cakes and tortes are spectacular; in fact, they won first prize for their chocolate truffle cake at the Chocolate Lovers' Fling. I say "they" because husband Jim now helps out in the bakery, and they also have another baker, named Tristan. Mousse cakes, quiches, flan, tiramisu–Linda likes to keep trying different things. And they're all from scratch, so check them out!

Karen's Country Kitchen

700 Main, Old Louisville 666-8020
Tuesday–Thursday, 6:30 am–8 pm. Friday & Saturday, 6:30 am–8:15 pm. Sunday, 8:30 am–1 pm.

Karen's started as a gift shop and bakery in 1974. Breads include cinnamon raisin, white and whole grain. Prices are very reasonable. Whole cakes, like chocolate carrot and German chocolate are only $9–$12, and cookies like white chocolate chip and Mom's gingersnaps are 35¢. Little butter cookies with chocolate on top are a little too sweet for my taste, but they have a cute name, "hugs and kisses". Gift items include Penelope's wine jellies, mustards and gourmet coffees.

Lick Skillet Bakery

5340 Arapahoe, Boulder 449-7775 Fax: 449-8271
Monday–Friday, 6 am–6 pm; Saturday, 7 am–5 pm;
Sunday, 7 am–3 pm. (Sunday, 8 am–3 pm in winter).

The story is that the head baker smuggled the sourdough starter for the pagnotta (Italian sour dough bread) in from Italy when she came back from her honeymoon two years ago. As well as the fabled pagnotta, you can get brioche here, muffins, stuffed focaccia, chocolate raspberry mousse cake, a delectable hazelnut cake with chocolate ganache icing and good tiramisu. Everything is made from scratch. Sandwiches are served, and everyone is friendly and helpful.

Manna Bakery

1500 W. Littleton Boulevard, Littleton 798-7117
Monday–Friday, 7 am–6 pm; Saturday, 7:30 am–5 pm. Closed Sunday.

Littleton doesn't suffer from a plague of too many bakeries, so it's refreshing to find this one, tucked in the back of a shopping center. They have a large variety of muffins: apple oat bran, banana nut, banana chocolate chip, mandarin orange, carrot walnut, peach bran and poppy seed, to mention a few. Fat-free muffins, like blueberry bran, are also available. They have cream and fruit pies, and specialty cakes like carrot cake, coffee cakes, napoleons and cream puffs. Their tortes look positively decadent: lemon coconut, butterfinger and oreo cookie torte. Breads include sourdough, seven grain, and honey wheat. Manna also has a variety of deli foods, including a very filling black bean and brown rice burrito, quiches, goulash, and Italian pasta salad. There's also bread pudding.

Pantry Basket

2423 S. Downing 733-0219
Monday–Friday, 6:30 am–4 pm. Closed Saturday & Sunday.

Stop in at this tiny bakery and lunch place for a big surprise! Apple or chocolate rugala, carrot cake, bow tie cookies, lattes, espresso, and pudding loaves, which are a cross between pound cake and bread pudding. Breakfast and lunch are served here, and they make a variety of breads, from whole wheat to raisin. Their cinnamon rolls are enormous.

Pete's Bakery

5600 Cedar   393-6247
Monday–Saturday, 7 am–7 pm; Sunday, 7 am–5:30 pm.

In a small neighborhood shopping center on Cedar and Holly, this little bakery is right next door to Pete's Fruits and Vegetables. It's also owned by Pete and surprise! Marilyn Callender, the chef from the late restaurant Mostly Seafood, is the baker. She's making pastries and desserts, and other wonderful edibles: for example, a veggie tart for $15, and gazpacho in summer. Pies, lemon bars, toffee bars, carrot cake...yumm! Breads are from Campagna, and not so expensive as they can be elsewhere. There are also some Greek pastries, as well as spanakopita (spinach pie) and tiropita (cheese pie) from Omonia, the Greek bakery on East Colfax. Coffee is also served here. Enjoy!

Scratch Baked

16400 S. Golden Road, Unit A. Golden   279-FRESH   Fax: 271-1880
Weekdays, 6:30 am–5:30 pm; Weekends, 8 am–2 pm.

The pies and tortes are simply gorgeous. Jerry, partner and head baker, often combines fruits or fruit and cheese, to make delights like strawberry rhubarb pie or pear cream cheese strudel. He has some good ideas, like country cakes that don't require constant refrigeration. Muffins, brownies, danishes, and flakers, made of sweet danish with cinnamon cream or raspberry filling, are available. Breads include semolina, honey whole wheat, six grain, three seed, pumpernickel and farmer's Bavarian rye. Jerry started baking in his basement, selling only wholesale, but his cakes, pies and breads are so beautiful, it's good he has a retail store to showcase them in.

Sugar-Less Sensations

6905 S. Broadway, Littleton   794-2753
Monday–Thursday, 7 am–6 pm. Friday, 7 am–8 pm;
Saturday, 9 am–8 pm; Sunday, 11 am–5 pm.

Pies, turnovers, scones, brownies, fritters–all with no sugar? Sounds too good to be true? You'll believe it at

Sugar-Less Sensations! Carol Morgan, herself a diabetic, wanted to make life tastier for others, and opened this attractive, guilt-free emporium! They'll make sugar-free cakes for all occasions, including wedding cakes. There are also many other sugar-free products here, including chocolates, fruit-sweetened catsup, fudge sauces and all-natural sweeteners made from fruits and wholegrains. Sugar-Less Sensations is an idea whose time has come. A big, sweet, sugarless smile for Carol Morgan!

Spruce Confections

2560 Pearl, Boulder   449-6773
Monday–Thursday, 7:30 am–6 pm; Friday, 7:30–4 pm.
Saturday, 9 am–4 pm. Sunday, 9:30–3 pm.

David Cohen didn't start out to be a baker. He was actually a composer who studied in Vienna and was student teaching at the Oberlin Conservatory when he was elected dessert baker in his food coop–and the rest is history. And a tasty history it is, with scones of many descriptions, shortbreads, cakes and cookies. He plans to start producing hand-made chocolates soon, so stay tuned!

Vollmers Bakery

7150 Leetsdale   322-7708
Monday–Saturday, 6:30 am–7 pm. Sunday, 7 am–7 pm.

Vollmers has moved from East Colfax to Leetsdale. The new bakery is very attractive, with a beautiful wall arrangement of breads and dried flowers behind the counter. The baked goods remain constant with breads of all descriptions: raisin, cinnamon and other sweet breads, whole wheat, pumpernickel, sourdough, egg bread and white. They have croissants and cookies, pies, coffee cakes and fruit stollen. Look for their many tortes, including their six layer lemon torte, which is one of their most popular. Their large variety of cheesecakes includes lemon, turtle and caramel pecan. The poppy seed log is one of their most unusual items. It has a rich poppy seed filling in a soft, sweet dough.

Asian Bakeries

Celestial Bakery, Deli & BBQ

333 S. Federal 936-2339
Daily, 9 am – 9 pm.

When I call to check on the hours at Celestial, the voice on the other end asks immediately, "Who are you?" The voice sounds about 8 years old. She's very quick and sure about the hours, however. When I arrive at the bakery, I find out she is Danna, whose uncle and aunt own this bakery and deli. They're serving dim sum items now, and there are pictures and descriptions on the back wall of various items: steamed barbecue pork buns, turnip cakes and pot stickers. There are also sweet dim sum items in the case, like sponge cake and sweet egg cookies. Or try a napoleon or other French pastry. Meanwhile, in the deli case, there are whole roast ducks hanging up, as well as an entire barbecued pig.

Korean Rice Cake O Bok Teok

9830 E. Colfax, Aurora 367-8989
Tuesday–Saturday, 10:30 am–6 pm. Closed Sunday & Monday.

Grace and Tom Min own this small but well-stocked bakery. There are several kinds of large sweet rice cakes, which should be cut into pieces for serving, and some round Japanese–style small rice cakes. All the bakery and noodle-type products are made of rice and sweet rice. Rice cakes with yellow beans can be used for main dishes or desserts. There are also cooked cylinders of rice that can be sliced and served with a hot and spicy pepper sauce or cooked in soup.

Vinh Xuong Bakery

375 S. Federal Boulevard 922-4968
Daily, 9:30 am–8:30 pm.

This dim sum bakery sells traditional dumplings served as dim sum for breakfast. They also have the largest almond cookies I've ever seen, as well as smaller almond cookies that are similar to shortbread, and two kinds of what I can only describe as Asian doughnuts. The round ones are covered with sesame seeds and filled with sweet yellow bean curd or–my favorite–coconut. The flat ones are plain. Their large, lemon-flavored cupcakes are also delicious. They have other desserts, like sweet rice, tapioca, and several desserts made with coconut milk. The best find of all, however, is the Vietnamese submarine sandwiches: roast pork or other meat with Vietnamese condiments on a crusty French roll– a very inexpensive and delicious lunch treat!

Bagel Bakeries

Bagel Brothers

7639 W. 88th Avenue Arvada 420-0990
Monday–Saturday, 6 am–6 pm; Sunday, 6 am–3 pm.

In a shopping center right off Wadsworth & 88th, Bagel Brothers brings in bagels from New York and bakes them on the premises. Poppy, sesame, wheat, apple cinnamon, muffins, with spreads like maple walnut, vegetable and health nut, in an attractive urban setting. They also have espressos, cappuccinos, steamers, sandwiches and breakfast bagels. Allegro coffee is sold by the pound, and the bagels to go are very competitively priced.

The Bagel Nook Bakery

6480 Wadsworth, Arvada 431-6311
Monday–Friday, 6 am–5 pm; Saturday, 6 am–4 pm. Closed Sunday.
The Bagel Nook South
7175 W. Jefferson, Lakewood 988-5926
Monday–Thursday, 7:30 am–3:30 pm; Friday, 7:30 am–3 pm.
Closed Saturday & Sunday.

If you're looking for a little Nooky, try the Bagel Nook or the Bagel Nook South. They both serve this specialty, which I'm sure they invented: a wiener or Polish sausage, wrapped in an egg bagel dough. It's then topped with cheese and baked (definitely not a kosher item!) There's a formidable variety of bagels, including plain, onion, sesame, poppy seed, wheat, garlic, pumpernickel, cinnamon raisin, egg, blueberry and sunflower–and an equally large variety of spreads: whipped butter, honey butter, cream cheese, cream cheese with chives, strawberry cream cheese, garden vegetable and wildberry, to name a few. They also have sandwiches, a pizza bagel, and brownies. In case that's not enough, there are pies, baked with fresh fruit in season, and cakes like carrot cake and New York cheesecake.

Bolo Bagel Bakery

1116 Thirteenth St, Boulder 440-9248
745B S. Colorado Blvd. 322-2966
Daily, 6:30 am–7 pm.

On the hill in Boulder, and now also in Denver, Bolo Bagel Bakery makes many kinds of bagels, from plain to poppy, sesame, garlic, cranberry granola and sun dried tomato. There are just as many spreads to put on them, like roasted garlic herb cream cheese, mango chutney, or Mediterranean. My favorite is the sun dried tomato spread. These bagels are chewier than most and cost $2.39 per 1/2 dozen or $4.49 for a baker's dozen.

The Bagel Store

942 S. Monaco   388-2648
Monday–Friday, 6 am–6 pm; Saturday & Sunday, 6 am–5 pm.

This is one of the few kosher bakeries in town. It's a little hard to find, in the back of a shopping center near the Monaco Inn. They've been in business for years, making bagels of all varieties: pumpernickel, rye, whole wheat, onion, garlic, poppy seed, egg cinnamon and raisin... They also make a variety of breads, like challah, pumpernickel, wheat and rye, and cakes, including banana nut cake, honey cake with raisins, and poppy seed cake. Cookies include mandelbrot and rugalach. Look for their new kosher doughnuts.

Dave–Pan Bagel Bakery

1907 S. Havana, Aurora   745-1154
Monday–Saturday, 6:30 am–4 pm; Sunday, 8:30 am–4 pm.

If you're looking for a hot cow, they have them at Dave-Pan. In case you're wondering what a hot cow is, it's hot pastrami, with lettuce, tomato and Dijon mustard. This is just one of Dave's deli sandwiches, and there are many more! Also as many different kinds of bagel as you could possibly imagine, almost, including egg, chocolate chip, raisin bran, garlic, onion, whole wheat, poppy seed, sesame, five grain, and, recently, pumpkin and blueberry too. They also have their own homemade chocolate chip cookies. Dave makes all his bagels fresh daily and also has bagel chips. They're addictive.

Finster Brothers

5709 E. Colfax (at Ivy)   377-2088 Fax: 377-1988
Daily, 6 am–3:30 pm.

Finster Brothers is a welcome addition to this area of town. Bagels of the poppy and sesame seed persuasion, sourdough, multigrain, egg, spicy pepper and even sweet things like oatmeal and cinnaraisin can be found within these walls. Spreads from lox or jalapeño cream cheese to Italian herb, blueberry and strawberry are available accompaniments. Add various coffee beverages, a smattering of sandwiches and a sweet touch of crumb cake, cookies or biscotti and voila! the fabulous Finster Brothers.

Heidi's Bagels & Ice Cream

3130 Lowell Blvd. 986-0602
Monday–Friday, 6:30 am–11 pm; Saturday & Sunday, 7:30 am–11 pm.
Closes earlier in winter.

The area around 32nd & Lowell is very lively and interesting, with a variety of delis, restaurants, crafts galleries and an occult store. Heidi's is a friendly, unpretentious place with bagels, ice cream, fresh bread, pies and sandwiches. Their bread is baked daily: French, Italian, whole wheat, sourdough–available to take out, and rye as well, but only for sandwiches. Bagels include all the usual kinds, with some interesting variations like orange poppy seed and "everything"–which sounds like maybe too much of a good thing. Pies like apple, peach, strawberry and rhubarb are almost all gone when I'm there. They must be pretty popular! There's sidewalk seating in the summer, and it's all very nice and neighborly.

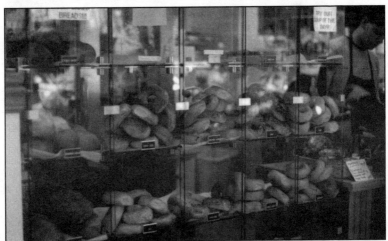

Jacobs Bagelry

290 S. Downing 744-6028
Monday–Friday, 6:30 am–3 pm; Saturday, 7:30 am–3 pm;
Sunday, 8 am–3 pm.

Everyone's so friendly and helpful at Jacob's and their goodwill and good humor is catching. Their many and various bagels include onion, garlic, poppy and sesame seed, as well as blueberry and bran muffins, and flavored cream cheeses to spread on them, like herb and spice, strawberry and walnut raisin. Specialty coffee drinks, like cappuccinos and lattes, are also available. They serve breakfast, which includes offerings like eggs with ham or sausage, and lunch, with sandwiches like turkey, chicken breast and BLT's. Just going into Jacob's is a pleasure–and the food is good, too!

Moe's Broadway Bagels

2650 N. Broadway, Boulder 444-3252 Fax: 444-2575
3075 Arapahoe Ave. Boulder 442-4427 Fax: 447-3072
550 Grant (6th & Grant) 733-7331
Monday–Friday, 6 am–7 pm; Saturday, 6 am–6 pm; Sunday, 6 am–5 pm.

Bagels, bagels and more bagels! Moe's has a wonderful variety, all delectable, from salt, tomato cheddar, pumpernickel and cracked wheat to cranberry walnut and cinnamon raisin. The cream cheese varieties to go with them are just as numerous, from whitefish to bacon and horseradish to garlic and herbs. Sodas and teas, juices, Celestial Seasonings ice teas, coffees, hot chocolate lemonade, cider... there's no lack of beverages to accompany bagels and sandwiches. Also, try the sun dried tomato spread or the pickled green tomatoes, and don't forget Moe's Bagel Chips.

New York Bagel Boys

6449 E. Hampden (Hampden and Monaco) 759-2212
Tuesday–Saturday, 7 am–6 pm; Sunday, 7 am–4 pm.

Walk into the New York Bagel Boys when they're pulling the bagels out of the oven and the smell is heavenly! The range of available bagel flavors is pretty amazing: from garlic, onion and pumpernickel to raisin and, on occasion, blueberry, and everything imaginable in between. They're all good, though I have a special fondness for egg bagels and whole wheat myself. Their bagels are made here, and have no added sugar. The fresh challah is some of the best in town, braided or regular loaves, with poppy or sesame seeds. You can also get bialys, Jewish rye and some cookies and pastries. Go into the New York Bagel Boys at Purim, which falls in the early spring, and give your taste buds a treat: hamantaschen. Shaped like the evil Haman's hat, these are pastries filled with poppy seeds and dates. They have fruit sticks and mandelbrot. This is a kosher bakery, and everything here is pareve, which means that it's made without milk or meat or their derivatives Everything's good here.

Danish Bakeries

Danish Delicacies

7475 East Arapahoe Road, Englewood 771-3314
Monday–Friday, 6:30 am–6:30 pm; closed Saturday. Sunday, 7 am–noon.

John Lundberg is actually Norwegian, but tries to encompass all the Scandinavian countries in his bakery. His homemade almond cinnamon raisin kringles and almond custard kringles are traditionally Christmas specialties, but available here all year round. Delights such as Danish butter cookies, strudels, danish pastries of course, rum balls with raspberries, rugalach, Sacher tortes, and Scandinavian whipped cream and marzipan tortes can all be found here. His breads include Julekage, a Scandinavian cardamom bread made with candied fruits and raisins, Swedish limpa, which is a rye bread, and others by request. At Christmas, he makes krumkake, a traditional rolled butter cookie and a Scandinavian special occasion cake called Kramsekake, made with almond paste, egg whites and sugar, and constructed in circles to form a kind of pyramid. Danish Delicacies has also expanded to offer a line of imported Scandinavian foods, including fish balls, mackerel, cod roe, pea soup, goat cheese, marzipan and lingonberries.

Caribbean Bakeries

Caribbean Bakery

2934 East Colfax   399-7993
Monday–Saturday, 9 am–8 pm; Sunday, noon–6 pm

Lance Huggins and Cleon McGregor run this little ray of sunshine on East Colfax. If you're ever feeling in need of a quick smile, walk in and listen to Lance talk with his wonderful, lilting Caribbean accent. Then try one of his almost magical drinks–my favorite is sea moss, although he does make mauby and others–it makes me feel like singing! Sweet breads like mango, coconut, and raisin, or whole wheat bread made with blackstrap molasses are singular and tasty. Coconut or ginger cookies, bread pudding or perhaps something more substantial, like one of their patties: ground chicken, ground beef or lentil (they're like pasties), or jerk chicken or even curried goat will give you a taste of the islands. This is the only Caribbean bakery in town, so make the most of it!

Eastern European Bakeries

Mama Pirogi's & Other Peasantries

2033 E. 13th Avenue   320-5608
Wednesday–Sunday, 7 am–6 pm; Monday & Tuesday, 7 am–noon.

Everything at Mama Pirogi's is made the old-fashioned way, with lots of time and loving care. Many breads and pastries are made from old family recipes, and all are traditional–not low-fat or low-sugar. There are a few tables where you can sit and sample a Russian tea cake or raspberry rugalach, or perhaps a lemon bar or some mandelbrot. The Russian tea cakes melt in your mouth. I can never resist them if I'm in the neighborhood. They also make kolache here, a Czech peasant bread from Eastern Europe, made with honey and poppy seed filling. Walter, the owner, claims to have the best carrot cake in the world. His Ukrainian poppy seed cake and toffee bars are equally well-loved. Walter also makes a breakfast pastry called schnecken, filled with poppy seeds and figs, and waxes lyrical about the traditional European way of baking. He certainly does a fantastic job of making things the old-fashioned way.

French Bakeries

Daniel's of Paris

12253 E. Iliff (at Peoria), Aurora   751-6084
Tues–Fri, 7 am–6 pm; Saturday, 9 am–5 pm. Closed Sunday and Monday.

Sinfully rich French pastries at rock-bottom prices. This is what you'll find at Daniel's of Paris. Lunettes (shortbread cookies pressed together with raspberry jam in between–they look like sunglasses, hence the name) are only $1 each, and napoleons, swan cream puffs and homemade creme caramel are equally well-priced. Try the raspberry mousse cake or the delectable peach melba cake, laced with a light Grand Marnier syrup, with raspberry filling, topped with sliced peaches and fresh whipping cream. Everything in the case looks so inviting, it's hard to choose just one, so enjoy yourself!

La Patisserie Francaise

7885 Wadsworth, Arvada   424-5056
Monday–Friday, 8 am–7 pm; Saturday, 9 am–6 pm. Closed Sunday.

This is the closest to a French patisserie you're going to find in Arvada! They make wonderfully authentic baked goods here, all cooked with lots of butter and sugar, all incredibly delicious and made with old-fashioned care. Apple and cherry

turnovers, apple or peach strudels, fresh fruit tartes, and lemon or almond sablé cookies, which are sweet and crumbly iced shortbread cookies. There's often a special of the week as well. One of these, a raspberry custard confection, is creamy, fruity tasting and unique. They have tortes, like cappuccino mousse or chocolate buttercream, and basilic, a chocolate cake with rum flavors, chocolate buttercream and raspberry. In the winter, there's a special treat called bustock–a bread pudding. And, of course, you can buy breads, especially French baguettes, here. One of Arvada's undiscovered treasures, La Patisserie Française is sure to please.

Le Délice

250 Steele 331-0972
Monday, 7 am–6 pm; Tuesday–Saturday, 7 am–9 pm. Closed Sunday.
Writer Square 446-0694 Monday–Saturday, 7 am–7 pm. Closed Sunday.

Since Le Délice opened their second bakery in Writer Square, there are two "very French bakeries" in town. They use no fat or sugar in any of their breads, and everything is made from scratch. Le Délice is owned by Maurice and Nicole Cochard. Maurice spent 11 years as the executive chef at Lafitte's, the very traditional French restaurant that was downtown in Larimer Square for many years. Their fresh fruit tartes, fresh charlottes, fruit mousse cakes and tartes lunettes–shortbread cookies filled with raspberry jam– are quite wonderful. Their boules and baguettes cause an immediate fit of nostalgia for small village boulangeries in France where people ride down the cobbled streets with crusty loaves sticking out of the baskets on the front of their bicycles. The loaves also taste just as delicious–crusty, fresh and flavorful. Le Délice in Cherry Creek has a small but interesting selection of French deli items: patés, creme fraiche (that wonderful, slightly sour cross between whipped cream and sour cream that's so hard to duplicate in the U.S.), French cheeses and European-style unsalted butter. This lovely little bakery serves meals as well. Its Writer Square cousin has sandwiches and salads to go, as well as all the delicious pastries and breads they have in the Cherry Creek store.

Le Français

2570 Baseline Road, Boulder 499-7429
Monday–Saturday, 7 am –10 pm. Sunday, 8 am –3 pm.

On a weekday morning, Le Français is abuzz with customers, sitting at the tables drinking coffee and eating pastries, chatting and having a good time. Looking more closely, I realize that many of them have grey hair. Perhaps this is a good place for unattached seniors to meet? Certainly, the breads and pastries are decorative enough to attract people of all ages and just looking in the pastry case could probably make us gain weight. But who can resist these brightly colored, fresh fruit tarts, or tartes citrons or mice made from sweet dough, filled with almond cream and chocolate mousse and covered with dark chocolate? Here they have four kinds of napoleon: vanilla, chocolate, strawberry and raspberry. Their whole fruit pies and tortes look spectacular, with a chocolate chocolate mousse cake that has a huge chocolate flower covering the entire top of the cake, or a Black Forest chocolate cake with whipped cream and cherries. I think this is a fine place for people of all ages to meet, and the crowd does change throughout the day. They serve espresso, wine and beer (although they call it expresso in the sign on the window–quel faux pas!) Oh, well! No-one's perfect.

Paris Bakery

1272 S. Sheridan 935-9353
Monday–Friday, 7 am–5 pm: Saturday, 8 am – 5 pm. Closed Sunday.

The baking brothers at Paris Bakery create all kinds of terrific tastes, at extremely reasonable prices. Breads like their boule, white or seven grain; sourdough and raisin breads, dark rye and, of course, their famous French baguette. Cakes and pastries like cream horns, chocolate bars, brownies, turnovers, cinnamon buns in several different incarnations and their singular open-faced strudels. The bakery has a few tables and chairs, so you can sit in comfort, have coffee and a pastry and enjoy the French country atmosphere created by the copper molds on the walls and the dainty lace curtains in the windows. The bread is always fresh, with a hard outside crust that contrasts delightfully with the soft inside. It's the way French bread should be. Coffee is available to enjoy with your pastry. This is always a good place to visit.

Sweet Soirée

4182 E. Virginia 388-3655 Fax: 399-4641
Monday–Friday, 7:30 am–5:30 pm; Saturday, 7:30 am–5 pm.
Closed Sunday.

This bakery specializes in French pastries and cakes, with tortes like basilica (chocolate and raspberry) or lemon tahiti, chocolate mocha and Frangelico. They also have cookies, meringue cases, breads, croissants, strudels and sweet rolls. Special occasion cakes are also available. Sweet Soirée is part of Le Petit Gourmet catering, so as well as their many varieties of baked goods, they also have soups, nut breads, hors d'oeuvres and quiches to take out and a complete catering and box lunch service as well. Some items require prior notice, but their on-site selection is large enough that you could easily drop in and pick up dinner or dessert if you don't feel like cooking. Combine hors d'oeuvres like duck in wonton, cheese and artichokes in brioche, or water chestnuts wrapped in bacon, with an entrée like beef bourguignon or beef strogonoff, accompanied by one of their fresh baguettes and followed by a couple of their fine pastries, and all you need is the wine!

TRIFLE

1 lb pound cake, cut into pieces
1 recipe instant lemon or vanilla pudding, made
    with 1-1/2 cups milk
1 pint raspberries, fresh or frozen (thawed)
Whipped cream
Sherry or rum to taste

Put the cut-up cake into the bottom of a large bowl (cut glass looks pretty, because you can see the layers of fruit, pudding and cake). Sprinkle with sherry or rum to taste. Pour raspberries over the top, including juice if they're frozen. Other soft fruit can be substituted, such as peaches or strawberries. Add pudding and top with whipped cream. Refrigerate for flavors to meld. Serves 6.

German & Swiss Bakeries

André's Confiserie Suisse

370 S. Garfield 322-8871
Tuesday–Friday, 9 am–5:30 pm; Saturday, 9 am–4 pm.
Closed Sunday & Monday.

André's is probably best known for their delectable pastries. Their lemon tarts simply melt in your mouth. Their strawberry kirsch tarts taste like fresh strawberries, right from the garden, with light cream and cake. Their tortes are suitable for the most elegant tea parties, kaffee klatches or dinner parties where you try (probably unsuccessfully), to pass them off as your own. André's also has a small but well-chosen selection of imported Lindt and Tobler chocolate bars, and a few Swiss products, like Knorr soups and mixes for making sauces for sauerbraten or beef bourguignon, and Lindt chocolate from Switzerland. Twinings tea would be the perfect foil for André's ultra-rich lemon tarts, fresh fruit tarts or linzer cookies. Their breads include gugelhopf, brioche and croissants. There's also a special fresh bread daily: Tuesday features sun dried tomato bread, Wednesday 8 grain, Thursday whole wheat, Friday potato and Saturday zopf, an egg twist. Quiches are available, either fresh or frozen, to take out, in flavors like cheese or chicken and broccoli. They also serve morning coffee, lunch and afternoon tea. André's is tucked away

in the just-off-Cherry Creek neighborhood. It's a little hard to find, but the pastries and breads are their own reward.

Das Meyer Fine Pastry Chalet

13251 W. 64th, Arvada 425-5616
Tuesday–Saturday, 7 am–6 pm. Closed Sunday & Monday.

Dennis and Elaine Meyer run this German bakery, housed in a country Victorian-style house, which you enter over a romantic hump-backed bridge. The bakery is right next to Morningside Manor, a wedding reception facility. Dennis has a case of ribbons and trophies for culinary awards–mostly for his wedding cakes. Inside the bakery, there are chintz curtains and a kind of rustic Victorian atmosphere. They offer rich pastries, including Black Forest cakes, dobisches (many-layered cakes with chocolate filling), cream and fruit pies and almond honey bars. They have changed some of their specialty breads, like their orange marmalade bread, and now make it with cream cheese. They always have several of these, like peach pineapple bread with cream cheese, orange swirl and cinnamon spiral bread. Attractive cakes, like napoleons, éclairs, lemon bars, several kinds of brownies and butter cookies sit temptingly behind the glass of the cases, begging to be boxed and taken home or eaten right there with tea or coffee.

Dimmers Home Bakery

2832 S. Havana, Aurora 751-8611
Tuesday–Friday, 8 am–6 pm; Saturday 8 am–5 pm. Closed Sunday.

Dasha Majer and her husband Paul own this attractive German bakery, and make everything with fresh ingredients and no preservatives. It's a genuine European bakery, where they take pride in their fine, old-country baking. The cakes and tortes are gorgeous–Black Forest and hazelnut, almond petits fours, éclairs, rum balls and assorted French pastries. German specialties include cherry strudel, chocolate marmork, streusel cookies, schweine ohren, linzertorte and bienenkuchen. They make their own fillings, like the poppy seed filling for the poppy seed roll and the fillings for the raspberry and apricot kuchen. Dasha and Paul have expanded their selection of boxed chocolates from Germany, Austria and Switzerland. And they have more imported candies and coffees as well.

Old Fashioned Bavarian Bakery

613 Frontage Road, Longmont 442-7121
Monday–Friday, 8 am–6 pm; Saturday, 8 am–3 pm. Closed Sunday.

"Rauchen Verboten", which means "No Smoking" says the sign above the counter. Michael and Helen–Helen doesn't give me their last name because it always turns out misspelled or mispronounced–have owned this bakery for almost eight years. They make both European and local pastries and German rye bread and the kind of hard rolls that are sometimes hard to find. Tiramisu, florentines, cream puffs, linzer cookies so delicious they melt in your mouth, napoleons, danish pastries (our pastry chef is Danish, says Helen). There's also a selection of different kinds of rugulach. The bakery houses a barbecue restaurant as well, but they can't resist offering some German specialties like roladen, chicken or pork snitzel and veal and smoked bratwurst with sauerkraut. This is a melting-pot kind of place, with one foot in the old country and one in the new. Chances are you'll find something here to strike your fancy. Guten Appetit!

Rheinlander Bakery

5721 Olde Wadsworth Boulevard, Arvada 467-1810
10354 N. Federal, Federal Heights 469-8572
8025 N. Sheridan, Unit U 427-5664
Monday–Saturday, 6:30 am–6 pm. Closed Sunday.

The award-winning Rheinlander Bakery now has three stores, offering the same European breads and pastries, like coffee cakes, fruit and cheese danish and schweine ohren (pigs' ears), and many other old-world baked goods. Ed and Maro Dimmer make their traditional bienenstich–a German coffee cake with honey and almonds, as well as Russian tea cookies, potica, an Eastern European cake with poppy seeds and walnuts, and even baklava. They make German rye bread, Swedish limpa and Jewish challah. The bakery produces many tortes, including mocha, marzipan, rum, Black Forest cherry and German chocolate. Their pastries are very good and very rich–all made with butter and the highest quality ingredients. The bakery was established in 1986, a second generation family-owned business. Edward and Maro Dimmer continue the tradition of Ed's parents, Jakob and Katharina Dimmer, who were famous for their rye bread, German tortes and pastries. They make special cakes for weddings, graduations etc. Cookies like streusel, cinnamon crispies and meringues are good too. The two newer stores (not the Arvada store) offer lunch sandwiches, and all the stores have specialty coffee drinks.

CHRISTMAS STOLLEN

Sweet Dough
7 oz butter
7/8 cup sugar
Pinch mace
1/4 tsp salt
3 medium eggs
1-1/4 pints milk
5-2/3 cups all purpose flour
3/4 oz dry yeast

FILLING
1 lb 6 oz diced fruits in any combination: orange rind, lemon rind, cranberries, pecans, almonds, walnuts, raisins. Fruit may be soaked overnight in 2 oz brandy or rum or combination, with a little honey
Marzipan (optional)
Unsalted butter, melted, for topping

Cream butter, sugar and add salt and spice. Dissolve yeast in 1/2 cup milk. Add flour and rest of milk. Knead till it forms a dough. Place fruit on work surface and cover it with dough. Knead until fruit is evenly distributed, about 5 minutes. Let dough rest on work surface covered with clean cloth. When it has risen to almost twice its size, punch down and shape into four rounds. If you want to add marzipan, flatten dough, spread marzipan and fold as though making an omelette. Roll over edge with rolling pin to seal. Dough will be soft. Rest 10–20 minutes. Bake at 325° on greased cookie sheet for 45 minutes. Immediately upon removing from oven, brush surface with generous amounts of melted, unsalted butter. Sprinkle with powdered sugar. Yield: four-1 lb loaves.

Rheinlander Bakery

CHRISTMAS BREADS
An ancient tradition

Bread is considered the staff of life in the European countries, and many of the bread-making traditions now associated with Christmas have even more ancient origins. In the Shetland Islands, Yule-brunies, a kind of oatcake, is still baked with edges pinched into points and a hole in the middle, witness to the ancient Scandinavian festival of sun worship. While everyday bread was coarse, festive breads call for use of fine and expensive ingredients, and many Christmas breads are so rich in fruits, spices and fat that they almost qualify as cakes.

These special breads survive even though most people no longer bake their own bread. Fruits were probably used originally because they were a method of sweetening, together with honey, before sugar was available.

Stollen   German Christmas Bread

The favorite Christmas bread of Germany, Weihnachts Stollen (Christmas bread) is widely believed to have originated in Dresden. Some people believe it should be as fresh as possible, while others insist that it needs to be stored for several days or even up to a few months for the flavors to marry before it's served. The shape is sometimes claimed to symbolize the Christ child wrapped in swaddling clothes.

Panettone Milanese   Italian Christmas Bread

Panettone is always part of an Italian Christmas. In December every year over 200 million of the packages are sold in Italy, and that's not counting the millions more that are exported all over the world. Panettone is seldom made at home. Probably the two most popular brands in Italy are Motta and Alemagna. According to Italian folklore, the recipe is a secret, but recipes appear in many books, and they vary in richness and complexity.

This high-crowned bread is reputed to have been created by a Milanese baker called Antonio, who improved upon Pan di Cherubini (cherubs' bread), a traditional Milanese sweet bread, in the hope of winning the hand of the girl he loved. It became famous as "Pane de Toni" (Tony's bread) and is baked at Christmas. It's also made at Easter, when it's made in the shape of a dove and called Colombo di Pasqua.

Rosca de Reyes   Mexican Three Kings' Christmas Bread

The person who receives the bean or doll baked into this cake is responsible for giving a party for all assembled on Candlemas Day, February 2nd. A version of this Three Kings' Bread is made in many countries: Germany, Holland, Portugal and France, as well as in Mexico. It has survived in the U.S. in Louisiana as King Cake. A cake is brought to work each week between Christmas and Mardi Gras. The person who gets the "baby" or doll in the cake has to bring the cake the next week.

Greek Bakeries

Omonia Bakery

2813 E. Colfax   394-9333
Monday–Saturday, 9 am–10 pm. Sunday, 9 am–8 pm.

Dino Karas, owner of this friendly little Greek bakery, makes yeasty French bread, as well as Greek Easter bread and Christmas bread (which are basically the same and available fresh at Christmas and Easter, frozen during the rest of the year). These holiday breads are made with eggs, milk, and fruit. His Greek pastries are various and delicious: baklava, kataifi, koulourakia, and galatoburiko. This last is a wonderful, rich, custard-filled pastry. Try the kasetina, a yellow cake with chocolate cream, dipped in chocolate. His cookies are rich and tasty, and he also makes custom wedding and other special occasion cakes. Omonia is a cafe as well as a bakery, so you can stop in for a pastry and coffee almost any time during the day. Dino makes spanokopita or tiropita (Greek spinach pie or cheese pie) for lunch or to take out. Greek coffee is always available, and the atmosphere is just like a small, European cafe.

Italian Bakeries

Breadworks

2644 Broadway, Boulder   444-5667
Monday–Friday, 7 am–7 pm. Saturday & Sunday, 7 am–6 pm.

Rustic breads are the order of the day–and there are several every day at Breadworks, a wonderful bakery in Boulder. Depending on the day, you may find the batard, pain de campagne, deli rye, green olive and sage, due formaggi (two cheeses) and many more. There are also fresh sweet baked goods, like muffins and scones, panini (Italian sandwiches) and several kinds of decadent brownies.

Campagna

1710 S. Broadway   698-9393
Tuesday–Saturday, 10 am–6 pm. Sunday, 7 am–4 pm.

When I walk in, it feels as though I just stumbled into a quaint old Italian farmhouse. The quality and uniqueness of the bread depends on imported European ovens equipped with steam injection, to give the breads a crisper crust. These rustic breads are truly delicious, especially the pugliese (Italian country bread), the sun dried tomato garlic and the honey wheat. Other specialty breads include ciabatta, chocolate cherry, and kalamata olive loaf. Campagna has cakes and cookies, as well as a selection of Italian cheeses and other deli items.

European Bakery

Marketplace Shopping Center at Bergen Park
1153 Highway 74   674-2825
Monday–Saturday, 7 am–7 pm; Sunday, 7 am–4 pm.

This lovely little bakery, packed with all kinds of European baked goods, has a thriving takeout business into the bargain! Breads include focaccia, whole wheat walnut, sun dried tomato basil, baguettes, ciabatta, and Italian country. All these are available every day. Semolina bread, challah and jalapeño cheddar are sometimes available. In case that's not enough, there are carrot and cheesecakes, fruit and custard pies, bagels, croissants and a number of cookies, including bowties–apricot or raspberry; florentines, almond paste cookies, rainbow cookies and scones. For takeout, look for pizza, calzones, seafood salads, mozzarella salad (it looks marvelous!) and lots more. Family size spaghetti includes garlic bread, salad, sausage and meatballs, with dessert, to feed 4–6 people, for $19.99.

Gargaro's Italian Bakery

5058 Marshall, Wheat Ridge   424-9881
Tuesday–Friday, 10 am–6 pm; Saturday, 9 am–3 pm.
Closed Sunday & Monday.

Gargaro's is in one of the most unlikely places for a bakery, off the beaten track about a block north of I-70 in a small, converted house. But don't be fooled! While I am here, a steady stream of customers arrives, to be greeted like old friends, choose their breads, pastries and other goodies, and walk out of the door happy as clams. And no wonder. Gargaro's prices are so reasonable, it would be hard not to be satisfied. Twist bread, cinnamon rolls, cookies, and biscotti, as well as sausage, cooked homemade pasta and tomato sauce, all very inexpensive. What a find!

GARLIC PIZZA CRUST

5 cups unbleached flour
1/2 cup polenta (coarse corn meal) or regular corn meal
1 tsp salt
1 Tbsp sugar
1 Tbsp olive oil
1 tsp very finely chopped garlic
1 pkg fast rise dry yeast
2 cups hot (125°) water

Preheat oven to 375°. Mix all ingredients except water until thoroughly blended. Slowly add water till a soft dough forms. You may not need all the water. Knead well until soft and elastic but not sticky. Brush lightly with olive oil. Place in a bowl, cover tightly and let rise in a warm place about 45 minutes, until doubled in size. Punch down. Let rest 5 minutes. Spread on floured table into a square or round shape, depending on shape of your pan. Sprinkle with flour and roll evenly to 1/4" thick. Place on pan that has been previously sprayed with nonstick spray or light olive oil. Trim edges with knife. Poke all over with a fork. Lightly cover with plastic wrap. Let rise about 10 minutes or until slightly puffy. Bake about 5–7 minutes to "par" or partially bake so it doesn't get soggy later. It may or may not turn brown. Top with your favorite pizza topping.
Phil Jones, Rosso's Ristorante, Red Lion Hotel

Nonna's

1920 Market Street, inside Bella Ristorante 297-8400
Mon–Fri, 7:30 am–close; Saturday, 9:30 am–close; Sunday, 8:30–close.

Walk into Bella Ristorante, an Italian restaurant downtown, and Nonna's is right inside the door. Breads baked fresh every day include ciabatta, onion fennel, and semolina. Other breads include honey whole wheat walnut, roasted red pepper with sage and sun dried tomato. The pastries and cakes have less of an Italian flavor: lemon bars, giant brownies, éclairs, napoleons, cookies and scones. Bagels and biscotti abound, as do specialty espresso coffee drinks. Sandwiches and box lunches have an Italian bent, with chicken pesto salad and tomato mozzarella basil sandwiches as two of the offerings.

Mexican Bakeries

La Favorita

2925 W. 38th Avenue 477-9658
Monday–Saturday, 8 am–8 pm. Closed Sunday.

This place is really popping just about every time I go in. There's Mexican music going in the background, people are ordering at the counter, and sitting at the tables in the restaurant waiting for their food. Through it all, the staff manages to be quick and friendly. I admire them. Come here for fresh La Favorita tortillas, corn tortillas and chips, as well as Mexican baked goods. Gorditas, tamales, burritos, green chile and other Mexican-food is available to eat here or take out. They have a selection of Mexican specialty ingredients like masa mixta, which is used to make tamales, corn husks to put the tamale mix into, ground chile, and an enchilada mix, among other things. To add to the feeling of bustle and happiness, bright, multicolored paper flowers nod their heads from giant baskets on the top shelves.

Mexidans

2101 Larimer 295-1773
Daily, 8 am–6 pm.

Mexidans has undergone a facelift since Coors Field opened, and it's very attractive inside, with small tables of wood inset with Mexican tiles. The baked goods feature a variety of sugary pastries, looking inviting in pastel rows behind the glass. Mexican breads, or bolillos, have a nice crust and just the right touch of sweetness. The carnitas are pork, cooked to a chewy crust on the outside but tender and flavorful within. There are tamales, for $6.25 a dozen, or $3.50 a half-dozen, and burritos, menudo, tostadas and enchiladas. All these are for takeout or eating in the newly renovated restaurant. Corn husks and chiles are available here too.

Panaderia Aguas Calientes

9075 E. Colfax 340-2594
Daily, 8 am–6 pm.

At first, this looks like a fast food Mexican restaurant, even though it says panaderia, which would lead one to suppose it's a bakery. I'm hesitant about going in, not liking to make a fool of myself, but once inside, I'm really glad I did! There's a whole bakery case, hidden from the windows, and everyone is so helpful and pleasant that it's a pleasure to be here! And, even better, the bakery and restaurant is owned by Miguel, who used to work at Mexidans. He's still making his great carnitas and burritos, and all kinds of other Mexican dishes. Also, the waitress is patient and helpful with me and takes the time to tell me the names of all the cookies: grajeas (sprinkles), campechanas (crispy), payasos (clowns), and escobas (brooms). This is a fairly new place, and prices are very reasonable. Give them a try.

Panaderia El Alamo

3165 W. 38th Avenue   477-8114
Daily, 6 am – 8 pm.

The only remaining evidence that this was once an Italian bakery is the crusty Italian bread, which is still made here along with the Mexican bolillos. There are Mexican-style pastries and cookies, such as polvorones, rieles, which means "rails", (they're long and thin) and orajas. Rum cakes and wedding cakes can be found here, and there's a wall of shelves with Mexican food products, like jars of nopalitos (cactus paddles), and other specialty items. Tortilla presses and molcajetes, the primitive-looking mortar and pestles used to grind chiles, corn and hominy, are in evidence. Most intriguing, I find instant jamaica tea mix–it's made of hibiscus flowers, and has a lovely rose color–and it's really easy to make and quite refreshing.

Panaderia Guadalajara

2223 W. 32nd Avenue   477-9916
Daily, 7 am – 8 pm.

Panaderia Guadalajara is a small bakery with a restaurant in the back room. Saturday and Sunday they serve menudo, and according to Francisco Lara Jr, son of Francisco Lara the owner, there's often a line at the door. The bakery offers a wide selection of pastel colored Mexican cookies and pastries. Tamales, carnitas and barbacoa are all available to eat here or to go. Their tamales are overstuffed with shredded pork and spicy sauce. They're some of the tastiest I've tried. The pumpkin candy they make right here in the store is extremely sweet and sticky. A charming custom in all the Mexican bakeries is to put your choice of goods on a tray with a pair of tongs, so that you can see exactly what you're buying. Then, when your purchases are complete, they're all put into a bag. Mexican baked goods are very different from French or other European cakes or cookies. They are sweet and flaky, and often drier than the butter-rich European baked goods. Panaderia Guadalajara is one of several Mexican-style bakeries in this neighborhood. Try them out and experience their unique tastes and textures.

Panaderia La Chiquita

6185 E. 72nd Avenue, Commerce City   286-1980
Daily, 7 am – 9 pm.

All the pretty Mexican pastries are here in the display case, waiting for hungry customers to come and claim them. But there's so much more, as well! Big bags of red chiles for just $5, spices like canela (cinnamon), manzanilla (camomile), and even chickweed and marigold, as well as chile chipotle: dried, not canned, and atole, a drink made of corn that originated with the Aztecs. It's made from ground corn, and sometimes flavored with chocolate. There's candy made of cactus, sweet potato and squash, and on weekends tortas, which are Mexican sandwiches. One weekends also, you'll find menudo, which is a kind of soup made with tripe; and carnitas. These carnitas are pieces of tender pork, fried till they're crisp on the outside, but still moist and flavorful inside. This bakery has a good price on wonderful instant jamaica (hibiscus) herbal tea. It's a very nice place.

Panaderia & Pasteleria Santa Fe

750 Santa Fe Drive 571-4720
Daily, 7 am – 10 pm.

Just before Lent, I come into this lively bakery and restaurant looking for carnitas with their tasty pico de gallo, and I notice that they have nopalitos in the grocery case. Nopalitos are cactus paddles, and these are fresh, already cleaned of their nasty little needles and cut up, which is a vast improvement on their natural state! Someone in front of me buys some, so I ask her how to cook them. Not always available, they're delicious as a Lenten dish, steamed like a vegetable or cooked in soup, as my fellow–customer explains to me. Don't miss the bolillos, or the great selection of desserts, pastries and other goodies. The oatmeal here is particularly good (I know that sounds odd, but it's true. It's very creamy–I think they put some tapioca in it.) In the refrigerator case I find Mexican specialties like crema mexicana, chorizo and ranchero cacique cheese. Chile and tamales are available to eat in or take out, as is the entire restaurant menu. This is a place full of good energy, in a very alive and interesting neighborhood.

Panaderia Rodriguez I

6201 W. Alameda, Lakewood 232-5646
Panaderia Rodriguez II
2402 W. 32nd Avenue 455-1405
Panaderia Rodriguez III
4044 Tejon 455-9394
All open daily, 7:30 am–10 pm.

At all the Panaderia Rodriguez locations, there are cakes for sale that look like individual layer cakes, creamy icing layered with a kind of pound cake/sponge cake, called pastelitos. These are not in all the other Mexican bakeries. They also have the usual Mexican-style cakes and cookies, all very fresh and attractive-looking. The range of their baked goods doesn't stop there: they also have cream cheese danishes, pineapple and apple empanadas, polvorones, raspberry flautas and other goodies. The cream puffs are called patos (ducks) because of their shape. They also have deli food, or "comida rapida"–Spanish for fast food– burritos, tamales and sandwiches, called tortas, of Mexican bread with ham or chorizo and cheese, and gorditas, which are hand-made tortillas, stuffed with different combinations of meat or chorizo, beans, chicharrones and green chile. Tamales to go are $7 a dozen. Luis, the son of the owner, explains to me that all their bakery goods are made fresh daily and that they also sell tortillas and tostadas. These are very nice bakeries, one of my favorites in the Mexican-style bakery category.

Pasteleria del Norte

2643 W. 32nd Avenue 433-5171
3637 W. 1st Avenue 937-8272
Daily, 6 am–10 pm.

Pasteleria del Norte has just opened a second bakery at West 1st Avenue and Meade. Their breads and pastries are inexpensive. There are also different kinds of cookies, including cinnamon and honey cookies, and empanadas (turnovers) filled with apple, cheese or pumpkin. They have red and green chile to go, pork rinds and an assortment of colorful piñatas. There's a rack of Mexican spices, with a large assortment, including cumin and manzanilla, and rosa de castillo (rose of Castille) which is small rosebuds. They also have cans of chipotle chiles in adobo sauce.

Rosales Mexican Bakery

2636 W. 32nd Avenue 458-8420
Daily, 6:30 am–10 pm.

What fun! This panaderia has an amazing array of colorful Mexican cookies and pastries, all for 20–75 cents each. They have marranitos, so-called because they're shaped like little piggies, and are made from a kind of gingerbread, and escobas, meaning brooms, which are flaky sugar pastry. Their cacahuates or peanut cookies are also named after their shape, and they're cookies in peanut-shaped halves, held together with an ample paste of frosting. Mexican candies are to be found here, too, with wonderful names like "grenudas"–haystacks, or, as the owner describes it, "hair messed up". There's also Mexican fudge and cubiertos calabaza, another kind of candy. Mexican products like nopalitos, masa, canned guavas, hominy and Ibarra Mexican chocolate line the shelves, and most interesting of all are the giant pinatas on the topmost shelves. I've never seen any quite this huge anywhere else!

Sexy Bakeries

Le Bakery Sensual

300 E. 6th Avenue (6th & Grant) 771-5151
Monday–Friday, 9:30 am–6 pm; Saturday & Sunday, 10 am–4 pm.

Le Bakery Sensual continues to provide fun, interesting and ingenious baked goods and candy for our delectation. John's decorations can be explicit, funny or romantic, according to your taste. The idea book showing some of his greatest hits will give you a starting point for bachelor or bachelorette parties, anniversaries, special birthday parties, over-the-hill parties or even children's celebrations. John says he's been providing more humorous cake designs recently, and has noticed an upsurge in depictions of people enjoying their favorite sport–golf, tennis, skiing–naked. He has been creating his humorous and erotic masterpieces for the last twelve years and is glad to put together any kind of cake or candy you can imagine. The card and gift department has been expanded because of increased demand. There's a children's section with toys and games to keep the little dears away from all the erotica while parents shop. An interesting piece of trivia: 95% of the customers here are women. Makes you think, doesn't it?

Delicatessens

Deli food is fabulous when you don't feel like cooking but you're too tired to go out to eat. Just stop by one of these places and pick up something quick and flavorful and presto!–there's dinner. We often think of deli food as European food–sausage, cheeses and prepared foods from the old countries, but we have a Mexican deli in Denver, as well as several Asian delis (see Mekong under Markets and several of the Asian bakeries). Fairly new to the area are Polish delis–and they've arrived in force. No less than four have opened within the last year. So discover the joy of not cooking–at the deli!

American Delicatessens

East Coast Italian Deli

8998 E. Hampden Avenue (Hampden & Yosemite)   741-0908
Monday–Friday, 7 am–7 pm; Saturday, 7 am–5 pm. Closed Sunday.

Tucked away in a shopping center at Yosemite and Hampden is the fresh and tasty East Coast Deli. It's a little hard to find, but persevere! The bowls in the deli case are filled with fresh salads daily, and they vary with the season. I think the variety here is great, with offerings of deviled eggs, spring salad, seafood and tabouli salads and an interesting variation–spaghetti salad–spaghetti noodles with Italian dressing and red onions, cucumbers and tomatoes. In the winter, they offer great homemade soups, which change daily. Meats available to take out by the pound include bologna, capicolla, liverwurst, pastrami, salami, turkey and roast and corned beef. Desserts are all homemade and include peach cobbler, rice pudding, apple crisp and chocolate surprise. The surprise is less of one than you'd think: it's made with vanilla and chocolate puddings, oreos and chocolate chips.

Mortensen's Gourmet-To-Go

5270 E. Arapahoe Road   773-6326   Fax: 773-6064
Monday–Friday, 7 am–5 pm. Open for parties on weekends.

Chef and owner Paul Mortensen graduated from the Culinary Institute of America, then worked in France and New York before moving to Colorado. He has breakfasts, salads, sandwiches, and all kinds of other gourmet take-out and catered foods. Appetizers include shrimp tossed in pesto with sun dried tomatoes and focaccia with pesto, olives and sun dried tomatoes. There are canapés like smoked turkey and brie, and cucumber with smoked salmon mousse. Quiches, beef wellington, lemon bars, brownies, mini-éclairs and cookies are some of the other offerings here. Discover calzones and enchiladas to go, as well as box lunches and other dishes you can pick up straight from the freezer. Paul offers a large variety of cuisines in his catering: Mexican, American, Italian and French. You can get almost anything delivered, too–for example, corporate breakfasts of various kinds: Continental, blintze and crepe breakfasts, are available for a minimum of six people. If you have special ideas in mind, call first to make sure Paul has what you want, or have him send you his extensive list of possibilities!

Rockies Deli & Bakery

1630 Welton   892-5802
Monday–Friday, 6:30 am–3 pm; Saturday, 8 am–1 pm.
Closed Sunday.

The muffins at Rockies–blueberry, chocolate chunk or country apple, among others, would make a breakfast by themselves. They also sell bagels, including garlic, salt, pumpernickel and honey oat; Boar's Head meats, like pastrami, turkey breast, ham and corned beef, and side dishes like potato salad and cole slaw. They serve breakfast and sandwiches, soups and salads for lunch and also offer catering. Around the corner, on the Sixteenth Street Mall, is Rockies Cafe, which shares a bakery with Rockies Deli, and is owned by the same people, Jim and Nancy Turley. The cafe has espresso and cappuccino, and some different items that I didn't see at the deli. They also sell coffee beans. Service is very nice and friendly at both places, and everything is fresh and wholesome-looking.

Star Market Deli & Catering

2357 E. Evans (Evans & University)   777-0495
Monday–Friday, 8 am–6 pm; Saturday, 9 am–4 pm. Closed Sunday.

Star Market used to be an old supermarket, back in the days when there were neighborhood markets. If you're looking for out-of-this-world carrot cake, this is the place to visit! They make their own carrot cake, banana bundt and poppy seed cakes, as well as their own chocolate cake topped with chocolate chips. But the carrot cake is my favorite. They have subs, salads and chili and the usual deli meats and cheeses. Star Market does catering and box lunches. There's fresh produce, juice and sodas and some grocery items. This is an eat-in or take out deli near DU. Stop in if you're in the neighborhood.

European Delicatessens

European Delights

8440 W. Colfax, Lakewood 237-5655
Monday–Friday, 10 am–6 pm; Saturday, 10 am–5 pm. Closed Sunday.

Marian Balaz is a man who loves to feed people. Seems as though everyone who walks into his deli on West Colfax gets a taste of one or the other kind of sausage–and he makes a lot of different kinds. His Polish sausage is full-flavored and very good, but his garlic sausage is simply outstanding. He also has hunter's sausage, Hungarian cabai, made with paprika and spices; liver sausage and home-smoked bacon with the rind still on. Everything is wood-smoked in the old way, with no preservatives, and less fat and salt than you would find in ordinary commercial products. There are some other European products, like Turkish coffee, smoked sprats and several different kinds of cookies. The praline wafers look delicious, and are made in a round shape, topped with chocolate, that has to be cut in wedges. There are also huge jars of honey, and jars of pickles and peppers. This is a family business, with Marian's wife Margaret (who's a seamstress–ah, those old-world skills!) and his daughter helping out in the deli when they can. They're from the republic of Slovakia, which used to be Czechoslovakia. There's a display of Bohemian crystal on one wall that's really beautiful. Stop by and enjoy.

German Delicatessens

Alpine Sausage Company

1272 W. Alaska Place 778-0886
Monday–Friday, 9:30 am–6:30 pm; Saturday, 10 am–4 pm. Closed Sunday.

You'll find so many kinds of sausage at Alpine Sausage, you'll have a hard time choosing which to take home. Each kind of sausage is tasty and different from the next. Bratwurst, knackwurst, bockwurst, chorizo, andouille, apple saucisson, potato, landjaeger, even Portuguese linguesa. Everything I've tasted from here is delicious. Bertram Frei is originally from Switzerland, and he's been making sausage for over 20 years. If you want to know about sausage, he can tell you about all the different kinds, how they're made, what goes into them, etc. He's just started making a new kind called saucisse aux choux, a sausage from the French part of Switzerland near Lausanne. It has cabbage in it. They also sell Roggenbrot, a German rye bread, and kaiser rolls. You can get sandwiches to go here, with 1/4 pound of sausage and choice of mustard for around $2.

Bender's Brat Haus

15343 E. 6th Avenue, Aurora 344-2648
Monday–Friday, 10 am–5 pm; Saturday, 10 am–4 pm. Closed Sunday.

Watching Chuck Bender make bratwurst is a treat. He makes it look so easy. Of course, he's had lots of practice. He's been making brats from an old family recipe for almost twenty years. They use all natural casings, and their brats are really delicious. Chuck says that two people working together can make about a hundred pounds of brats in an hour. They make their own sauerkraut here, too, as well as German potato salad and also a krautburger sandwich consisting of ground beef, cabbage and onion. They sell the brats both cooked and ready to eat and take-it-home-and-cook-it-yourself. To take home they're $3.19 per lb and there are usually five brats per pound. Homemade side orders are $13 per gallon for potato salad and $17 per gallon for cole slaw. A few kosher dill pickles to go with, and who could ask for more? If you want to wash your brat down with a beer, that's possible at Bender's, since you can eat at the restaurant as well as take out. This place is totally unique. The people are wonderful and the food is good, straightforward and inexpensive.

Continental Delicatessen

250 Steele 388-3354
Monday–Friday, 9 am–5 pm; Saturday, 9 am–4 pm. Closed Sunday.

A surfeit of sausages is what you'll find here: knackwurst, bratwurst, veal brats, frankfurters, wieners–all freshly made. Their hams include bauernschinken, bierschinken and prosciutto, and they have Westphalian weinwurst and imported cheeses, like Jarlsberg, French raclette, Edam, and Quark, the famous German soft cheese, which is rather like a sharp ricotta or cottage cheese. Unusual ingredi-

ents include raw poppy seed and sweet butter, as well as many varieties of dark German deli breads. I've never seen such a complete selection of Knorr soups, bouillons and mixes, from bearnaise and lyonnaise sauces and sauerbrauten and bouillabaisse spices to dessert mixes like chocolate mousse and soufflé. There are many kinds of preserves and jams, and more unusual spreads like chocolate hazelnut spread, rose hip preserves from Switzerland and acacia honey. Thank goodness, there are also many different varieties of mustard. I find a fine selection of European chocolate, mostly made by Tobler and Lindt, and large jars of chocolate coffee cordials on the counter. Intriguingly, there are several products available in tubes, such as mustard and mayonnaise, which I find very useful and easy to use.

Helga's German Delicatessen

728 Peoria, Aurora (Hoffmann Heights Shopping Center)   344-5488
Monday, 8 am–8 pm; Tuesday–Saturday, 9 am–9 pm;
Sunday, 11 am–8 pm.

If you love things German, including the atmosphere, visit Helga's. The hams and sausages are many and various, and include bauernschinken, liverwurst, schinkenspeck, Westphalian ham and touristen wurst. I have unpleasant visions of this last item as something horrid, perhaps made of tourists, but I'm reassured by hearing that it's just a salami-type sausage. The landjaeger is more of a smoked, jerky-like sausage, and nuss-schinken is smoked ham. You can find several kinds of herring at Helga's, and as well as the deli case there's a shop full of German and Austrian delights, like mixes for potato pancakes and potato dumplings, Maggi brand "fix für sauerbraten" or schweinebraten, or even rouladen, and lots of different teas and coffees. Eiernudlen are egg noodles, and there are packets of spaetzle which look delicious, judging from the pictures on the front! Quark, that German cheese that makes terrific desserts and cheesecakes, is here. A German friend of my cousin's once made us a dessert from Quark the last time I was in England, and it was quite heavenly. Several kinds of cookies: apfel (apple), orangen, kirsch and marzipan, line the shelves, and there are lady fingers too. There's a mix for rotegrütze, a very special fruit dessert, and also several mousse mixes. Helga's dessert case is filled with incredibly delicious-looking confections. In fact, I believe I put on a few extra pounds just standing next to them. Black Forest torte, hazelnut, lemon, raspberry or rum torte, homemade cheesecake or apple or cherry strudel with whipped cream all look too good to pass up.

Karl's F.F. Delicatessen

6878 S. Yosemite, Englewood 694-0260
Monday–Friday, 9 am–5:30 pm; Saturday, 9 am–3 pm. Closed Sunday.

Karl and Ursula Boschen are the owners of this bright and cheerful German deli. There's a fine variety of German sausage and ham displayed in the deli case: blood-tongue, head cheese, liverwurst, Schwarzwalderschinken, knackwurst, wieners and more. The shelves loaded with German products prove interesting. There are many kinds of German mustards, including some usefully packed in a tube, as well as pickles and sauerkraut. Look here for lots of luscious-looking German jams and preserves, syrups such as raspberry, blackberry and sour cherry, and herb teas like chamomile, rose hip and peppermint. There are imported sweets, European chocolates like Lindt and Sarotti, marzipan, and mixes for lemon, chocolate and strawberry mousse. There are also some German creams and lotions, including the European version of Nivea, which some of my European friends still prefer over the American version. Karl's has a patio if you want to sit out and enjoy the sun while eating, if the weather cooperates. In fact, in spite of the "FF"-fast food–Karl's manages to evoke a pleasant and leisurely European sidewalk cafe.

Omi & Pa's

2049 Wadsworth, Lakewood 274-6468
Monday–Saturday, 8 am–7:30 pm (summer); 8 am–6:30 pm (winter).
Closed Sunday.

Runza by any other name would still taste...like runza. There are variations, but it's basically ground meat with potatoes, cabbage and cheese inside homemade bread dough. Omi & Pa's used to be known as the home of the runza until a company in Nebraska informed them that runza was their trade name. Now they call it Meister Run, which somehow isn't quite the same. There are many other choices at Omi & Pa's, in any case, or in this case, in the deli case: bierkaese, for example, which is like stuffed bacon, or fleischkaese, which is a bologna-type meat but spicier. There's also a smattering of sausage, like smoked brats, knackwurst, and bockwurst. They make their own spaetzle here, and also their own side salads. On the shelves, you'll find rose hip, chamomile and hibiscus teas, German mustard and sauerkraut, red cabbage with apple and herring fillets. Desserts? Jawohl! Streuselkuchen could come in apple, plum, strawberry or peach, and they make their own carrot cake and cheesecakes. Bienenstich and cream horns are available too. This is a homey and welcoming place, named by Omi & Pa's grandchildren. (Always dangerous, to let the kids name the joint.) Omi and Pa are their pet names for their grandparents, so it works for them!

Italian Delicatessens

Belfiore's Italian Sausage

3161 W. 38th Avenue, Denver 455-4653
Monday–Saturday, 8:30 am–5:30 pm. Closed Sunday.

If you're in the neighborhood, stop in and visit with Teresa. She has homemade hot and mild Italian sausage, as well as homemade fresh pasta: gnocchi, ravioli and tortellini. Their Italian cheeses include Romano Pecorino, Asiago, and imported provolone. There's salami, pepperoni, olive oils, Italian lupini beans and sweet roasted peppers. You'll also find a selection of imported dried pastas, balsamic vinegar, bread sticks and biscotti, and Perugina chocolates. I really love the frozen desserts, made of puff pastry and filled with cream. Take some home and bake them in the oven. Dreamy!

Carbone Italian Sausage

1221 W. 38th Avenue   455-2893
Monday–Saturday, 8 am–5 pm. Closed Sunday.

Carbone's has been supplying the old Italian section of North Denver with sausage and other Italian delicacies for over 50 years. They make their own sausage, and it's delicious. There's also Calabrese salami, sopressata, capocollo, Genoa salami and other meats, as well as cheeses like fontinella, scamorza, locatelli, provolone, goat cheese and Italy's most famous cheese, Parmigiano Reggiano. The production of this hard, tasty cheese is heavily regulated, and it must be aged at least two years. Along the top of the counter are many kinds of peppers, brightly colored and fresh-looking in jars. In the refrigerator case, John's brand gourmet pastas include manicotti and ravioli, among others. There are olive oils and vinegars, and many different shapes of La Molisana and De Cecco pasta. Carbone's has just started making deli sandwiches, like Italian sausage or prosciutto and cheese. Check out their lunch menu!

PESTO A LA VICTORIA

- 1–6 oz can black pitted olives, drained
- 1–6 oz jar green Spanish olives, drained
- 1–6 oz jar marinated artichoke hearts, including marinade
- 1 head garlic
- 1 oz (8–10) sun dried tomatoes

Peel garlic. Add to olives, artichokes and tomatoes. Mix thoroughly. Simmer in sauté pan 45 mins or until garlic is tender. Purée in blender to coarse paste. Use over pasta or warm on Italian bread.

Karen Gruda

Cucina Leone

763 S. University 722-5466 Fax: 698-2055
Daily, 9 am – 9 pm.

Plus ça change, plus c'est la meme chose, as they say in France. Which is to say, the more things change, the more they stay the same. This is certainly true at Cucina Leone, where pastas, pizzas, salads, and entrées change every couple of months, but always stay tasty, innovative and delicious. Entrées might include spicy rubbed and slow-roasted baby back ribs, or fresh chicken breast saltimbocca, layered with prosciutto and mozzarella with an olive, caper, artichoke and tomato salsa. Pizzas could be Napoletana: thin crust, light sauce, light cheese and fresh basil, or Fiorentina: creamy fresh spinach, pancetta, wild mushrooms and caramelized leeks. Salads could be simply wood-grilled fresh vegetables with balsamic vinaigrette glaze (divine!) or fire-roasted red peppers with capers and extra virgin olive oil. The food here is exceptional, so just about anything you choose will be delightful. Don't hold back. Order a side of roasted garlic mashed potatoes if available. Or indulge in their scone pudding or other bread pudding options, or their rice pudding. Reserve the chef's table for yourself and your friends, and work with chef Jack Leone to design a wonderful and memorable meal. Breads, desserts and coffee are also available here, courtesy of Aspen Baking Company, bringing you everything from baguettes to desserts and coffee. The concept behind Cucina Leone is restaurant quality food to take home. You can eat there, and the surroundings are certainly quite lovely, but why not make off with the goods and eat at home with your shoes–and any other articles of clothing that might be chafing after a long day–off?

Deli Italia

1990 Wadsworth 238-7815 Fax: 238-7815
Monday – Saturday, 9 am – 6 pm. Closed Sunday.

There's always something new and interesting at Deli Italia and Ricardo is always delighted to talk about it! We look at a new line of pasta, which includes a shape called cicatelli–cigarette ends. There are also dollar signs (verdoni) and orecchiette (little ears) and strozzapret (strangle the priest). Bretelloni are suspenders. There's an amazing variety of pasta, including an entire section devoted to pasta for soup. My favorites are in the shape of little hearts. Deli Italia has one of the very best selections of olive oil and balsamic vinegar in the city, as well as several varieties of Italian tomatoes in cans, and in boxes. There are also boxes, trademarked Pomi, of soup: bean or vegetable. Cheeses are wonderful: Parmigiano Reggiano, Asiago, imported provolone, mascarpone, and, if you're lucky, some of Ricardo's handmade mozzarella, rich and creamy with just a hint of smoke, lovingly crafted into the size of a tennis ball, fresh and delicious. He makes it every day, but it's so popular that sometimes they run out. Italian sausage, soppressata, pancetta, prosciutto and porcetta beckon from the deli case. Ricardo tells me about the porcetta, how delicious it is sautéed with basil and tomatoes, served over pasta. I vow to make this dish as soon as I can, and take a slice of porcetta, which is made of two pork loins, wrapped with pigskin and pressed together. Porcetta is from the region around Rome, explains Ricardo, and although you can get it with less fat, it doesn't taste as good. He doesn't bring it from Rome, however, but from an Italian company in Canada. Several kinds of olives are available, including a great olive salad. On my way out, I spare a loving glance for my favorite non-alcoholic aperitifs, in the drinks case. They are wonderfully various, mostly rather bitter, and a sophisticated alternative to almost any kind of drink at almost any time of day. Deli Italia also has a good selection of cookies, biscotti, ladyfingers and other sweet things. Cappuccino and espresso? But of course.

Lonardo's Italian Sausage Meat Deli

7585 W. Florida, Lakewood 985-3555
Monday–Saturday, 8 am–6 pm. Closed Sunday.
15380 Smoky Hill Road, Aurora 699-4532 Fax: 699-6945
Monday–Friday, 9 am–7 pm; Saturday, 8 am–6 pm. Closed Sunday.

Carmine Lonardo is from Campobasso, 150 miles east of Rome. He's been in business over 15 years. Big wedges of Asiago, Parmesan and Romano jostle ricotta and Gorgonzola in the refrigerator section of the Lakewood deli. There are also many fresh pastas, like tortellini, ravioli, manicotti, and even gnocchi, and fresh-made chorizo as well as hot and mild Italian sausage. Carmine and his family sell quality fresh meats, like steaks and chops, in small quantities or as one of several bulk packages of meat or meat, poultry and sausage.

These package deals are posted above the counter, with prices. You can also buy capocollo and sopressata and other Italian meats, and several kinds of fresh Italian bread. There are many rows of peppers in jars: hot, mild, cherry, roasted and in various other incarnations. Also there are marinated mushrooms, Italian giardiniera, and a good selection of olive oils from Colavita, Carapelli, Bertolli and Celio, among others, as well as several kinds of balsamic vinegar. If you have a sweet tooth, don't pass up the Perugina chocolates or various Italian cookies.

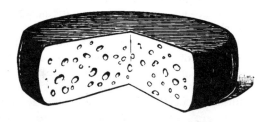

Old Fashioned Italian Deli

395 W. Littleton Boulevard, Littleton 794-1402
Monday–Friday, 8:30 am–7:30 pm; Saturday, 9 am–6:30 pm.
Closed Sunday.

In addition to their fabulous oversize sandwiches, with names like the Terminator and the Destroyer, because you probably can't finish them before they finish you, the Old Fashioned Italian Deli now serves pizza, by the slice or whole. Greek salads and subs are also good–as is their raspberry lemonade. For dessert, try some bread pudding (plain, $1.50) or with peach brandy sauce, whipped cream and a cherry for $2.50. This is a special, so they may not have it every day. However, they also have tiramisu, so there's always a sweet ending–if you can find room after one of those sandwiches. You can also find stuff to take with you like salami, pepperoni, cheeses and a large variety of imported pasta, as well as olive oil and balsamic vinegar. What you won't find there anymore is Tom, the Old Fashioned Italian Deli's guiding light, and an all-round wonderful human being. He's gone back to New York to be an air traffic controller (which was his profession before the strike–remember that?) He'll be back when he retires. We hope it won't be too long, but meanwhile his kids are running the place. Perhaps he's onto something as a way of keeping his kids out of mischief!

Roberto's Sausage

1415 E. 58th   297-0370
Monday–Friday, 6 am–4 pm. Closed Saturday & Sunday.

Sausage–hot or mild Italian and German–is made fresh on the premises with no additives or preservatives. There's also turkey, roast beef, capicola and braunschweiger. At lunch, there's a variety of sandwiches, with a different special each day. All the specials are under $4 and there's nothing on the entire menu over $5. Choose from an Italian hoagie, capicola, corned beef, or a beef or bean burrito. The Thursday special is the most unusual: an Italian egg roll, with mozzarella, sweet chili peppers with Italian sausage and fried in an egg roll skin for only $1.49. Desserts include cheesecake, brownies or cookies. Roberto's caters to the surrounding industrial neighborhood, and it's always busy at breakfast and lunch. Marvin Feist, the owner, is friendly and helpful. He also offers catering, with deli trays, box lunches and 3 or 6 foot long subs!

Salvaggio's Italian Deli

2609 Pearl, Boulder   938-1981   Fax: 938-1987
Monday–Friday, 10:30 am–9 pm; Saturday, 10:30 am–8 pm; Sunday, 11 am–6 pm.

Derek Estabrook, who owns Salvaggio's with his partner, Steve Salvaggio, describes the place as an East Coast-style deli. When I ask what that means exactly, his manager, Jim, quips, "Good food, bad attitude". But he's wrong. They have a very good attitude here, with everyone obviously enjoying the place, and pitching in to make it work. There's capocollo, prosciutto, salami, as well as roasted red peppers, several kinds of olives and specialty salads like potato, tortellini, and artichoke and corn. They have subs, soups, salads and make all their breads from scratch. Voted best deli by the Boulder Daily Camera, this is not just a meal, it's an experience.

Tony's Italian Sausage and Deli

3855 Wadsworth, Wheat Ridge   420-1557
Tuesday–Friday, 10 am–5 pm; Saturday, 10 am–4 pm. Closed Sunday.

The most unusual thing about Tony's is that they have homemade frozen foods to take out, all from grandma's

Italian recipes. These include meatballs, lasagne and Calabrian wedding soup. Tony and his family make their own hot and mild Italian sausage, and they have a selection of meats and cheeses, like salami and prosciutto, Parmigiano, Romano, fresh mozzarella and imported locatelli. Parsley, oregano, black pepper and basil are some of the spices that are available in flat plastic containers, and there's a good variety of pastas, mostly imported, like La Molisana. You will also find canned Italian tomatoes, and large containers of red wine vinegar and olive oil. Italian coffee and the small espresso makers to make it in are here, as well as hot cannoli, stromboli, calzones and pizza, hot and ready to eat.

Valente's Deli Bakery

7250 Meade, Westminster 429-0590
Monday–Saturday, 8 am–5 pm. Closed Sunday.

You can now find fresh meats at Valente's, as well as the baked goods and deli and Italian products they've always had. Homemade Italian and hot Italian sausage in the deli case separates the fresh meats from the deli meats like capicola, prosciutto and sopressata. Cheeses include Asiago, Romano and Swiss. Breads range from the usual rye, pumpernickel and sourdough to English toasting bread and apple fritter bread. There are also home baked pastries. Noodles range from R&F to Molisana to de Cecco. A variety of sauces can be found, including the Classico brand and some spaghetti sauce from Valente's restaurant (the owners of the restaurant and the deli-bakery are related!) Bertolli's olive oil is featured here, in a variety of sizes. There are tables and chairs, so if you want to, you can sit down and stay awhile.

BASIC POLENTA

2 cups enriched yellow cornmeal
2 cups cold water
6 more cups water
1 Tbsp salt

In a medium bowl, mix cornmeal and 2 cups cold water with a fork to a smooth paste. In a heavy, 5 quart saucepan, bring 6 cups water to a boil. Add salt and cornmeal paste to the boiling water, stirring constantly with a long wooden spoon. Bring mixture to a boil. Turn heat to low. Cook the polenta, stirring frequently to keep mixture smooth, till very thick, about 30 minutes. It should be so thick that a wooden spoon will stand unsupported in the middle. Cooked polenta can be poured onto a buttered platter and served with a tomato-based sauce. or poured into a well-buttered casserole, covered and allowed to cool to room temperature.
                    Cosolo's Italian Market

Jewish & Kosher Delicatessens

The Bagel Delicatessen

6217 E. 14th (14th & Krameria) 322-0350
Monday–Friday, 7:30 am–5 pm; Sat & Sun, 8 am–5 pm (8–3 winter).
6439 East Hampden (Hampden & Monaco) 756-6667
Mon–Fri, 7 am–8 pm; Saturday, 8 am–8 pm; Sunday, 7 am–7 pm.

There's always a welcome at the Bagel Delis, run by Joe and Rhoda Kaplan. You'll find all manner of tasty Jewish food to take home or eat in the restaurant. All the Jewish delights you can imagine are here: matzoh ball soup, knishes, corned beef and kosher salami, homemade chopped liver, kosher pickles, lox, smoked fish and cream cheese; herring salad, egg salad, fresh fruit salad and much, much more. They do, of course, have bagels, English muffins and egg bread, and they also have chocolate mousse cake, apple or cheese strudel, lemon pound cake, carrot cake and even flan! You can buy borscht and bologna, mozzarella and Muenster, roast beef, corned beef, halvah and blintzes. Gefilte fish is also available, along with that great horseradish colored with beet juice that always goes with it. If you're looking for tasty, home-style Jewish food, the Bagel delis are the place to go.

East Side Kosher Deli

5475 Leetsdale 322-9862
Monday–Thursday, 8:30 am–9 pm; Friday, 8:30 am–2 pm;
Sunday, 9 am–7:30 pm. Closed Saturday.

This is a nice place to shop for baked goods and Jewish specialty items. It's a restaurant but you can also buy quantities of homemade kosher specialties to take home. Several different kinds of kugel: apple raisin noodle, onion noodle, carrot or potato; kosher deli meats like corned beef, pastrami, roast beef, and don't forget the side dishes, like their famous potato salad, pasta salad, and three bean plus salad. Everything is kosher. Call ahead and order sliced brisket, sweet and sour meatballs, matzoh ball soup, or cakes, turnovers or strudels. If you hanker for gefilte fish with horseradish, it's here. There are all kinds of kosher meats, salad dressings, and borscht, delicious beet soup, often served cold in Jewish households with a dollop of sour cream. I also find tabbouli, couscous and kasha, as well as sweet lemon and Jaffa orange marmalade from Israel. The apple dumplings are terrific, and all their baked goods look fresh and wonderful. Mel and Irma Weiss run this busy place with great energy and goodwill. Come by to shop or sit and eat. Just remember, they're always closed on Saturday!

New York Deli News

7105 E. Hampden 759-4741 Fax: 759-5055
Monday–Thursday, 7 am–10 pm; Friday & Saturday, 7 am–11 pm.
Sunday 7 am–10 pm.

In southeast Denver, there's a little bit of New York. At the New York Deli News, you'll find knishes, kreplach and mushroom barley soup. corned beef, pastrami, tongue, brisket, chopped liver, and kishka. The bagels are boiled in New York water, and sent to Denver to be baked. They have nova lox, whitefish, sable fish, gefilte fish, borscht, matzo ball soup, challah and blintzes. Their desserts include chocolate killer cake, New York cheesecake, apple strudel, and black and whites–halfmoon sponge cakes, iced half in chocolate, half in vanilla. They now make all their desserts right here. For a taste of New York without the trash and the traffic, try the New York Deli News.

Plaza Deli

2456 S. Colorado 756-5489
Monday–Friday, 7 am–8 pm; Saturday, 7 am–6 pm;
Sunday, 10 am–3 pm.

Some things never change, and thank goodness for that! One is the fabulous chopped liver at the Plaza Deli. They make all their own salads, like tuna and chicken salad, and cook their own brisket and roast beef. Their hot winter soups are all homemade: chicken, matzo ball, kreplach, and barley and beef. And they have a bread pudding that's positively addictive, served with a sweet and tart lemon sauce. I'm assured that the rice pudding is equally splendid, but will have to wait for another time to try that! The Plaza Deli has changed a little over the years, of course. There's a low-fat menu for diet-conscious customers, offering all lean corned beef, low calorie chicken and tuna salad, a healthy salad with turkey breast, tomatoes, onions and cucumbers. There are also cole slaw, three bean salad, and cucumber salad, made with oil and vinegar dressing, and pasta salad with low calorie Italian dressing and fruit salad with low fat yogurt. I still love the old black-and-white photos on the wall from the Jewish Historical Society. One is of a group of people outside the Denver Ice Cream Brick and Dainty Company. Dainties are 1 cent and Bricks are $1. That's a while ago!

Rosen's Deli

3921 W. Colfax 623-7690
Monday–Friday, 11 am–4 pm. Closed Saturday & Sunday.

Rosen's might win the prize for deli that has changed the least in its fifty years of existence. You can buy Jewish deli items by the pound, including corned beef, pastrami, roast beef, nova lox, stuffed kishke, chopped liver, kosher liver sausage, and knockwurst. The sodas in the case and along the back wall look as though they may have been there for fifty years. There's a Dr. Brown's soda in a celery flavor that I've never seen before. Sandwiches are available too. The kosher chili bowl is only $1.75, and you can watch the soaps on TV while you eat! For a quick trip back in time to Denver's west side Jewish neighborhood, go to Rosen's.

Zaidy's Deli

121 Adams 333-5336 Fax: 333-4118
Monday–Thursday, 7 am–8 pm. Friday, 7 am–9 pm.
Saturday & Sunday, 8 am–9 pm.

Zaidy's relies on old family recipes and ultra-fresh ingredients to make this kosher deli special. Zaidy means 'grandfather', so if you want a meal like you'd get at grandpa's this is the place. They have the usual lox, smoked sable and white fish, as well as corned beef, roast beef, salami and pastrami. Their soups are all homemade, and include vegetable barley, matzo ball and chicken soup with kreplach. Homemade knishes, chopped liver and cheese blintzes rival the potato latkes (pancakes) and matzo brei in popularity. Desserts include fruit and nut pies, cheesecake, Boston banana cream pie, coffee cake, carrot cake and lemon coconut cake with chocolate frosting–all homemade. I had one of the best corned beef sandwiches of my life at Zaidy's. It was lean and tasty, with a generous pile of flavorful, folded meat with a lean, slightly salty flavor, just the right amount of condiments, on fresh rye, soft in the middle with a bite in the crust and a crisp pickle. I hear their reuben sandwiches are out of sight as well. Breakfast or brunch is time to sample Zaidy's challah French toast or homemade cheese blintzes or even kippers and scrambled eggs, which sounds more English than Jewish to me! Zaidy's comes to us courtesy of Gerard Rudofsky and his son Jason.

Mexican Delicatessens

Lala's Gourmet Mexican Deli

3609 W. 32nd 455-1117
Monday–Friday, 11 am–7 pm; Saturday, 10 am–4 pm. Closed Sunday.

This is a family operation, run by Lala and Zeke Lucero and their son, Santiago. Lala is famous for her tamales, which come with pork or in a vegetarian incarnation. Red and green chile is available to go, as well as several terrific salsas. Tinga, a kind of shredded barbecued turkey, is made fresh on the premises, and it's delicious. Carne adovada is also hot and tasty, rice, beans and guacamole are available in pints and half pints, and chorizo, longaniza, carne adovada and tinga are sold by the pound. Chipotle peppers are one of the great treats to be found at Lala's, as they make their own. They're very sweet and not as hot as those you get from the can. Delightfully different! I'm also partial to Lala's flan. Because everything's made fresh from scratch, they sometimes run out of some items. Call first if you have your heart set on a particular thing. There are tables, so you can eat here as well as take out. This whole area at 32nd & Lowell is a lovely little district of shops, coffeehouses, art galleries and restaurants. Spend some time in the neighborhood. There's a lot to see.

POSOLE

About 1 lb boneless pork, cut into cubes
2 Tbsp olive oil
1 large onion, preferably red or white, chopped
3 cloves garlic, crushed
2 cups canned white hominy, rinsed and drained
2 cans condensed chicken broth plus 1 can water
2 Tbsp crushed red pepper
1 Tbsp dried oregano
1 tsp ground cumin

Sauté pork and onion in olive oil over medium heat until pork is no longer pink. Add garlic, pepper, oregano, cumin, chicken broth and water. Simmer 25 minutes or until pork is tender. Add hominy. Cook 10 minutes. Serve with tortillas or corn bread. Serves 4.

Polish Delicatessens

European Gourmet

6624 Wadsworth, Arvada 425-1808
Tuesday–Thursday, 10:30 am–6:30 pm; Friday, 10:30 am–5 pm;
Saturday & Sunday, 11:30 am–3:30 pm. Closed Monday.

Behind the counter, sausages hang just like they used to in the old country. "It took a while to make the health department understand that these are dry sausages, and this is the best way to display them," smiles the owner, watching two small, serious blonde maidens run back and forth from the back room to the counter. As well as the sausages, (czoshkowa with light garlic, jalocona with juniper), he has a selection of Black Forest and Westphalian hams. There are mixes for barscz (borscht) and for several kinds of pudding called kisiel. Desserts figure large in the inventory: cookies, wafers and lots of wonderful European chocolate. In the refrigerator case, pierogi with meat, cheese or sauerkraut cosy up to Bavarian farmer's rye bread. Syrups like gooseberry, red currant and raspberry try to outshine jams like pear, chokeberry, blackberry and gooseberry. Marinated yellow peppers are next to red peppers stuffed with cabbage. And in the fish department, look for sprats, smoked eels and mackerel in tomato sauce. I think rosehip spread is the most unusual item in the store until I spot Playboy in Polish. Do they have Polish playmates?

Nina's Deli

5050 S. Federal, (Broadway & Federal) Littleton 347-8077
Tuesday–Saturday, 9 am–8 pm; Sunday, 9 am–3 pm.
Closed Monday.

If you're a sucker for sausages and partial to paté, you'll be nuts about Nina's. Her paté is veal and quite delicious, not to mention inexpensive. Polish sausage is also very tasty, and there are delicacies like braunschweiger, hunter's sausage and and Westphalian ham. She has oodles of noodles. There are big boxes of chocolates that seem like a good deal, as well. There are several kinds of European chocolates, in fact, and other kinds of sweets, like strawberry candies. Marzipan cake is quite unusual, and there are jams and syrups too. Teas, pearl barley, poppy seeds and whole cleaned marjoram and paprika can be found here. Polish stuffed cabbage is a specialty of Nina's. Take some home.

Staropolska Deli

2720 S. Havana, Aurora 337-5210
Tuesday–Saturday, 10 am–7 pm; Sunday, 1–4 pm. Closed Monday.

According to Irene, who is the owner of the Staropolska Deli, she has Hungarian salami, as well as Czech and Russian, 50 kinds of Polish sausage, every single one different, 4 kinds of head cheese, cheeses from Holland and Switzerland, 12 kinds of herb tea, including blackcurrant, horsetail and St. John's wort, many kinds of fish, including 4 kinds of herring, 3 kinds of bacon, and 2 kinds of caviar. There are Polish pierogi (dumplings) and pelmeni (stuffed noodles or dumplings), many kinds of sweet cakes and pastries, including ginger cakes, poppy seed rolls, chocolate-covered nut cake and bobka, a poppy seed loaf. And then we get to the jams, and the sauerkraut, borscht, red currants in syrup, and, deliciously different, blackcurrant juice and a wonderful drink from Australia of all places–Walkabout soda. The kiwi has the freshness of green apples and is simply divine.

STUFFED CABBAGE LEAVES

1 lb ground beef or beef & pork
1/2 minced onion
1/2 cup cooked rice
1 Tbsp chopped fresh dill
1 Tbsp chopped fresh parsley
Salt & pepper
2–3 cups good spaghetti sauce, preferably homemade
Optional: 1 T sugar & 1 T vinegar, for a sweet sour taste

Sauté meat and onion in a pan. Drain fat. Mix with rice and herbs. Season to taste, adding sugar and vinegar if desired. Parboil 8–10 cabbage leaves in boiling water for 1–2 minutes each. Put meat mixture in middle of each and fold like a little parcel, folding ends inside. Tie with thread or secure with tooth picks. Place seam side down in baking dish and cover with spaghetti sauce. Bake at 350° for 45 minutes. Serves 2–4.

Tedi's Polish Deli & Buffet

6510 Wadsworth, #220, Arvada   423-4870
Tuesday–Sunday, 9 am–9 pm. Closed Monday.

Tedi's is a cheerful place, run by Teresa and Diane–hence the name. You can sit down and eat here, stuffing yourself with pierogis and Polish sausage, sauerkraut, cabbage rolls, potato pancakes and other Polish pleasures, or you can shop at the quite extensive deli/market, where dried sausage, hams, head cheese and other delights await you. Polish music plays as you examine the teas, mustards, canned fish like oysters and sardines, and in the refrigerator case, such things as farmer's cheese, beef strogonoff and several kinds of Polish cake. Pierogis are available by the half dozen or dozen. Boxes of chocolates are surprisingly inexpensive, and kisiel puddings are interesting. The closest thing I've had to kisiel is cornstarch pudding, except kiesels are thickened with potato starch and made with water instead of milk. The taste is delicate–sort of a cross between jello and pudding. They come in flavors like pineapple and cherry. There are also many yummy jams and preserves that would taste great on almost anything.

Pasta

Pasta Pasta Pasta

278 Fillmore, Cherry Creek 377-2782
Monday–Friday, 10 am–5:30 pm; Saturday, 10 am–4 pm.
Closed Sunday.

This is a great little place, discreetly tucked away off a patio in Cherry Creek North. Patti and Lisa Miller make all their own pastas. Egg and spinach and ravioli are available all the time. Fresh pasta by the pound and pasta dishes and other delicious creations are available to take out or eat at one of the tables in the restaurant. On any given day you might find one or two chicken dishes and one or two pasta dishes available in the case. Some of their most popular selections include chicken milanese, pasta with spinach and tomato, meat lasagne and veal cannelloni. Italian meatloaf is also a frequent people-pleaser. Desserts often include cassata, a Sicilian chocolate cake made with pound cake, cream, fruit and chocolate; lemon squares, key lime pie and sometimes ricotta cheese pie. This is one of the best places in town to visit when you don't feel like cooking. You can pick up an entire meal, or just some fresh pasta and serve it with your own wonderful quick sauce.

For fresh pasta, see also Belfiore's, The Cheese Company, Cosolo's, Fratelli's and some Italian delis.

SPAGHETTI CON AGLIO E OLIO

1/3 to 1/2 pound spaghetti
3 plump garlic cloves, minced fine
5 tsp extra-virgin olive oil, or more to taste
Garlic salt and fresh ground pepper
Chopped Italian parsley (optional)
Crushed red peppers (optional)
Freshly grated Parmesan cheese

Bring abundant salted water to a boil. Stir in spaghetti. While the pasta is cooking uncovered, prepare the sauce.
Add the olive oil to a frying pan over low heat. Stir in the garlic. When bubbles first start appearing around the garlic, begin stirring it. Continue for three minutes. Don't let the garlic brown. Stir in the chopped Italian parsley. Remove pan from heat, but return it about a minute before adding pasta.
When pasta is al dente, drain it and toss it well in the warm pan. Season to taste with garlic salt, red and black pepper. Add grated Parmesan cheese and mix well. Transfer the pasta to warmed plate. Top with additional Parmesan cheese and serve immediately.
                              Dave Angelino, Denver writer

Specialty Meat & Fish

Cherry Crest Market

5909 S. University, Littleton 798-2600
Monday–Thursday, 11 am–9 pm; Friday & Saturday, 11 am–10 pm.
Closed Sunday.

There's something fishy going on at the Cherry Crest. A restaurant as well as a fish market, this is one of the best places in Denver to find fresh fish. When I'm there they have live lobsters, sea and bay scallops, shrimp, smoked salmon and fillets of salmon, tuna, sole, and orange roughy. There's a special North East style lobster and clambake offer which includes steamer bucket, live lobsters, fresh fish fillet, clams, new potatoes, and corn on the cob, all layered in seaweed for $44.95. It serves two. Check for seasonal variations in their offerings, but if you love fish, don't miss the Cherry Crest Market.

Dale's Exotic Game Meats

1961 W. 64th Avenue   657-9453
Monday–Friday, 7 am–3 pm. Closed Saturday & Sunday.

If you fancy a bit of pheasant, you might prefer partridge or want to go for geese–Dale's is the place to head for. You may have a little trouble finding it, but it's worth the effort. The entrance is just to the north of Smokey's Barbecue on the north side of West 64th Avenue. Dale's is one of the largest suppliers of exotic meats in the country, supplying restaurants and retailers with rattlesnake, alligator, pheasant, elk and other farm-raised exotic meats, making their own game sausage and hot and sweet mustards to go with them. Rabbit, antelope, black bear, beaver, lion, wild boar... all these are available. Even a whole goat, or portions of New Zealand elk, venison, or cuts of caribou and buffalo come from Dale's, whose motto is "Our business is going wild." Sausage from exotic meats, like rabbit and wild boar, or New Orleans andouille and boudin, can be obtained for those who crave the taste of the wild. Dale's also has many canned products, like venison in curry sauce, buffalo chili and elk or buffalo jerky. These are also available in gift shops, as Wild West treats.

Fred's Fine Meats

5614 E. Cedar   377-2979
Monday–Saturday, 7 am–7 pm; Sunday, 8:30 am–5 pm.

Fred and Clyde both worked at the Supersaver at 3rd & Holly before beginning their careers at Fred's. This means they've both been around as long as almost anyone can remember! Fred's offers dry-aged beef and lamb, homemade sausage and specialty items like frozen capons, duck and rabbit. There are always several kinds of kinds of fresh fish; also rotisserie chickens and barbecued chicken wings, cooked and ready to take home. Their meats are all top quality, and they will cut or cook any meat to suit your fancy. This is an old-fashioned butcher's shop with great products and service.

Herb's Meats & Specialty Foods

2530 Baseline Road, Boulder   499-8166
Monday–Saturday, 9:30 am–6 pm. Closed Sunday.

Herb's is a great find. There are all kinds of ready-marinated meats, as well as frozen prepared foods. Herb's elevates convenience to an art, without sacrificing quality. There are fresh marinated beef or lamb kabobs, Cajun pork, turkey schnitzel and chicken fajitas. Marinated Cornish game hens look delicious, as do the chicken breasts, marinated in teriyaki, Thai or honey Dijon dressing. Look in the frozen foods case for burritos, tamales, Mexican quiche, breasts of chicken wellington, alfredo or florentine, roasted green chiles, egg rolls and more goodies too numerous to mention. They make their own sausage at Herb's, including kielbasa, jalapeño, Italian–hot or mild–and bratwurst. Side dishes include rosemary roasted potatoes and four kinds of potato salad.

SAM'S TERIYAKI SAUCE

1 cup low sodium soy sauce
3 Tbsp sugar
1/2 cup mirin rice wine
2 oz Black Jack Daniels Bourbon
3 cloves garlic, mashed
1 tsp sesame oil
2" ginger root, peeled and cut
Pinch serrano chile (optional)

Mix ingredients in blender. Lay chicken thighs in glass baking dish and cover completely with marinade. Allow to marinate for slightly under an hour (otherwise it will get too salty). Barbecue on low grill, turning frequently so it doesn't burn. Marinade should be enough for about 15 chicken thighs.
                    Sam Arnold, The Fort Restaurant

Louisiana/Texas Catfish

3357 Downing 298-1920
Tuesday–Saturday, 10 am–7 pm. Closed Sunday & Monday.

Here you can buy fish to cook at home–cat fish fillets, red snapper, shrimp, and other goodies like Texas hot links, andouille and boudin. You can also have them cook it here to take out. Choices include cat fish, snapper, frog legs, chicken wings or drumsticks, onion rings, fried okra, pickled pig feet, and gumbo in the cold months. They also sell jambayala mix, Cajun étouffé mix, red beans and yellow grits. Desserts can include cakes, pies and cobblers. Supplies fluctuate, so call first.

Oliver's Meat Market

1312 E. 6th Avenue 733-4629
Monday–Saturday, 8 am–7 pm; Sunday, 9 am–6 pm.

Oliver's has acquired a big smoker, (I did that once–it was a big mistake!) and now offers great ribs, chicken, smoked brisket, chopped barbecued beef and chicken... in fact, they can handle almost any kind of smoking, including a whole pig. Geese and ducks are delicious smoked, because it gets rid of some of the grease. Oliver's also has Coleman and other high quality meats, including a full line of lamb, and unusual items like sirloin tip roast. They oven roast their own roast beef and turkey, with no preservatives or hormones, and make many different kinds of sausage; Cajun, brats, Mediterranean, all with no preservatives or MSG. Also, they're always so nice and helpful. This area contains Greens Market (right next door) and the Blue Point Bakery too.

Sam's Continental Meat Market

15445 East Iliff 696-6146 or 696-6159
Monday–Friday, 8:30 am–6:30 pm. Saturday, 9 am–6 pm. Closed Sunday.

Frog legs, crab legs, salami, bologna, German sausage, Italian sausage, breakfast sausage and bratwurst. If it used to walk, swim or crawl along the ocean bottom, you can find it at Sam's. T-bones, pork chops, stuffed crab, deli meats... and some marinades, sauces and mixes, like the Zatarain's mixes from New Orleans, guaranteed to make sure bons temps rouler at your house, cher!–including red beans and rice, dirty rice, shrimp creole and jambalaya. I like them. Although they're a little more salty than I would make myself, they do have that authentic touch of the bayou. And they're ready in about half an hour! Everyone at Sam's is very helpful, and it's a good place to buy quality meat or fish in this neck of the woods.

Sir Loin Meat Shoppe

1910 South Havana (at Jewell) Aurora 751-0707 Fax: 751-1706
Monday–Friday, 10 am–7 pm. Saturday, 9 am–7 pm. Sunday, noon–6 pm.

Sir Loin is an aristocrat among meat markets. Here you can find choice grade meats, and special order any kind of buffalo. Prepared foods like chicken Kiev or Santa Fe, chicken cordon bleu or Mexican-style, save on time and preparation. Twice-baked potatoes or other side dishes such as cole slaw, baked beans, mashed potatoes or seafood salad, seem appealing when making an entire meal is out of the question. Roast beef, pastrami, prosciutto are ready to eat, while more exotic meats like quail, rabbit or geese are in the freezer. Catfish, crawfish, tuna steaks, snapper and scallops are available, as are all kinds of sauces, chutneys, marinades and even fajita sauce, to make even the best meat or fish more flavorful. Desserts? Cookies and cheesecake by the slice.

Uncle Milt's Fine Meats

6235 E. 14th Avenue (at Krameria) 333-0806
Monday–Saturday, 9 am–6 pm. Closed Sunday.

Uncle Milt's specializes in homemade sausage, like bratwurst, Italian, and hot Louisiana links. They have choice grade meats and their chickens are all-natural. For me, though, the best finds here are the Zatarain's mixes. Zatarain is an old company from Louisiana that makes mixes like shrimp and crab boils and Creole seasonings. Uncle Milt's also has Paul Prudhomme's magic seasonings, so you can find quite a lot of the necessary ingredients to make quick and easy Creole/Cajun dishes.

Wally's Quality Meats & Deli

12755 W. 32nd Avenue, Wheat Ridge 232-5660
Monday–Friday, 9 am–6 pm; Saturday, 8:30 am–5:30 pm. Closed Sunday.

Nancy and Carl have taken over from Thea Weyher, and are continuing her tradition. Fine meats, dry aged beef, all choice, aged a minimum of two weeks, and always well-trimmed; homemade bacon and ham, and many gourmet basting sauces and marinades. There is also an amazing variety of homemade sausage: German, Polish, hot or mild Italian, chorizo, Sheboygan and Swedish potato. And don't forget, in the frozen foods case you can find linguisa, andouille, frozen buffalo patties and rabbit. There's a butcher on duty all the time here, so whatever your little heart desires can be accomplished. You can find homemade spaghetti with meatballs, baked beans with bacon, macaroni salad, and other delicious items too numerous to mention. Nancy and Carl put out a newsletter, with special offers and a chance to win a freezer package of meat. Be sure to get on their mailing list.

MOE'S CREAM CHEESE APPETIZER

16 oz cream cheese
1 tsp lemon juice
1 tsp Worcestershire sauce
1 Tbsp fresh garlic, minced
1 Tbsp dill weed
4 oz ground black pepper
More ground pepper for rolling in

Mix all ingredients together, except pepper. Add ground pepper. Form into a long thin roll. Roll in fresh ground pepper, chill and slice. Serve on crackers or toast points.
Moe Razi, owner of the former Café Montmartre

Cheese

The Cheese Company

735 S. Colorado Boulevard 778-6522 Fax: 778-1088
Monday–Friday, 9:30 am–7 pm; Saturday, 9:30 am–6 pm. Closed Sunday.

There are times in everyone's life when indulgence is the only option. And although we hear more and more about the evils of fat, there are times when a creamy Brie spread on a crisp baguette or a grating of fresh Parmesan or Asiago over a plate of noodles is no longer a luxury–it's a necessity. When these moments occur in your life, run, don't walk to the Cheese Company. Not only do they have all the wonderful cheeses your heart desires, they also have everything to go with–from water biscuits to baguettes. You can pick up pasta by the pound or one of many other delights, from wheatberry caviar to pasta chips to wonderful pasta sauce-style dips especially for dipping with crusty bread. If you are actually going to cook yourself, at least get a head start with Rowena's spicy hot peanut or curry sauce. Or have a sedate English tea, with lemon curd, raspberry curd or Robinson's ginger jam. If cooking is simply out of the question, take home some of the dishes from the takeout case. Chicken pasta Caesar might fit the bill, or chicken pecan feta or chicken breasts made one of a dozen ways, one or two of which are always available here. In winter, look for tenderloin stuffed with chili and cheese, polenta pie or one of the many other treats they have in store at the Cheese Company.

About Denver's Markets...

The proliferation of ethnic food in Denver was the inspiration for the Adventures in Eating series, and nowhere is this proliferation more evident than in the ethnic markets. I'm always amazed by the variety of products to be found in any one market. Don't be fooled into thinking that you'll just find Middle Eastern foods in a Middle Eastern market or Mexican foods in a Mexican market. Many of the Asian markets carry British products, Middle Eastern markets may carry some Italian products and many tropical ingredients can be found under a number of different ethnic names.

African Markets

Air–Afrik

4536 E. Colfax 393-0654
Monday–Saturday, noon–7 pm; Sunday, noon–6 pm.

Frank Chei is from Ghana, and he runs this small ethnic boutique, which has African clothing and crafts as well as food items. I would never have known about this place without the help of Peter Sarkoda of Herbs and Spices restaurant. Here you can find white corn meal, dried fish and shrimp, mackerel and sardines, plantains, potato starch, fufu flour and palm oil. There are also some English items, remnants, no doubt, of the far-off days when the sun never set on the British Empire. Heinz salad cream, Walker's shortbread and such items as tinned corned beef and baked beans are in this category. Another find here is the Stewart's ginger beer, much spicier than regular ginger ale, and twice as good!

Asian Markets

Asian Deli

2829 28th Street, Boulder 449-7950
Monday–Saturday, 10 am–8 pm; Sunday, 10 am–7 pm.

Billed on the takeout menu as "where Boulderites go for tantalizing Asian food" this place is more of a market with a restaurant attached than what we would normally think of as a deli. There are Indonesian foods here as well as Vietnamese: ketjap manis is one example, and there are Indonesian noodle crackers and curry mixes. In fact, there are a lot of mixes of all kinds, such as Korean barbecue, egg flower soup, golden curry and even a kim chee mix. There's also instant Vietnamese sour soup. Mud fish lurks on one shelf, and there are a number of chili sauces, hoisin sauces, sesame oils and hot chili oil. There's also an extensive Vietnamese takeout menu, as well as two or three tables for those who want to stay and eat. The menu is extensive and very inexpensive. Salads and vegetarian dishes are highlighted, and there's a large drink menu, including longans on ice and toddy palm & jackfruit on ice. Try one of these; they're called che, or, if you're not feeling that adventurous, have a Vietnamese coffee.

Asian Market

333 S. Federal 937-1431
Daily, 9 am–8 pm.

The first thing I notice in this large market in the Far East Center on South Federal is the two aisles of tins of assorted English-style biscuits (cookies to Americans!), some made in France, some from Indonesia, and Malaysia. There are gaufrettes, petit beurre and my favorite (at least for the name) strawberry cream-filled love rolls. There is also a selection called happy assorted biscuits. There are lots of different kinds of teas, including jasmine tea, and canned exotic fruits like longans and lychees. They have many of the same ingredients that I've encountered in other Asian markets, including hoisin sauce, sambals, hot chili sauce and a huge selection of canned fish, like crab, sardines and oysters. There are also lots of frozen fish and fresh fish as well, some of which are half-hidden in huge buckets of ice. In the frozen food section are won-

ton skins and eggroll wrappers. Here's where I find china tea mugs with lids and the kinds of plates and bowls often seen in Asian restaurants.

Durian (see left), a tropical fruit, is available in Asian markets, sometimes fresh and sometimes frozen. It's brownish-green and spiky, larger than a football, with an unattractive smell, but a smooth, creamy texture and a delicious taste.

Aurora Asian Market

15401A East Mississippi Avenue   750-5408   Fax: 750-4494
Daily, 9 am–9 pm.

There's more than foodstuffs to be had in this market, which has mostly Korean and Japanese ingredients. There's also jewelry, makeup, baby clothes and other dry goods that line one wall, as well as bowls, cookware and cooking gadgets. There are pine nuts, chestnuts, and walnuts, and many different kinds of tea, from arrowroot to green tea and ginger to honey citron. Big bags of rice of various kinds are piled up, and there are also mung beans and dried black beans as well as millet, rice flour in large bags, acorn and mung bean starch, fermented soy bean powder and dried malt powder. Buckwheat noodles, also called Japanese vermicelli, are among the many kinds of pasta, as is a Korean pasta made with potato starch. Most intriguing of all, however, are the bowls of panchan, appetizers or side dishes–whole pickled garlic, fish of various kinds and black beans. Right next to this are gigantic jars of kim chee of several kinds, including turnip greens kim chee. Meat, like beef oxtail and shank bone, is one of the few food categories to be labeled in English. There are several kinds of dumpling wrappers. Fresh vegetables range from lettuce, spinach and napa cabbage to several kinds of hot peppers, garlic, onions and several kinds of cucumber.

Denver Oriental Supermarket

10260 E. Colfax Avenue, Aurora   360-7444
Monday & Friday, 10 am – 8 pm; Tuesday – Thursday, 10 am – 7 pm; Saturday, 9 am – 6 pm. Closed Sunday.

Don't be dismayed by the fact that the front door to this market is locked. You can enter quite easily through the parking lot in the back of the store. This large market has at least ten different kinds of soy sauce, ten kinds of rice vinegar, ten kinds of fish sauce, and hoisin sauce, kung pao sauce, Szechuan chili sauce, big jars of hot pepper paste, black bean paste and soy bean paste. There are also big jars of honey, including cactus honey; corn syrup, malt syrup, hot mustard as powder and in tubes, and also tubes of wasabi. There are many soup mixes, including corn cream soup, anchovy bouillon, miso soup, instant seaweed soup and egg flower soup. Noodles include vermicelli, bean thread, chow mein and soba noodles. There are several different kinds of curry made by the same manufacturer, including Vermont curries with apples, and Java curries. Asian cookies and candies fill a whole aisle, and there are musk melon candies, plum, sweet bean jelly, coffee flavor and something called pineapple gummy. Teas are green, or made from roasted cassia seeds or pearl barley. There's something resembling a panchan bar here, with many different kinds of pickled fish and vegetables as well as kim chee. (Panchan are side dishes that are not kim chee.) The market provides toothpicks so you can try a little of each to make sure you like them before you buy. Many of the products in this store are not labeled in English. There are tables where you can order food and sit and eat it, but nothing is in English, so if you're feeling adventurous, order by pointing.

Indochina Enterprises

1045 S. Federal   935-0400
Monday – Thursday, 8:50 am – 7:30 pm; Friday & Saturday, 8:50 am – 8 pm; Sunday, 8:50 am – 7:30 pm.

Lots of boxes of assorted chocolates here, and at very reasonable prices, too. There's a fine selection of teas as well, including one labeled "relaxing tea". An incredible number of snacks and assorted candy, including banana snacks, yellow lumps of rock candy and my personal favorite for a brand-name–Palace Shack–preserved plums. There's canned Normandy butter and piles of noodles of all kinds. Palm sugar

DUMPLINGS WITH RED OIL SAUCE

SAUCE
1/4 tsp soy sauce
2 Tbsp peanut butter
1/2 tsp sugar
1/2 tsp salt
1/2 tsp chili sauce
Dash hot sauce
Dash vinegar
4 Tbsp water or chicken stock

Mix ingredients together

TOPPING
2 green onions, chopped
2–3 sprigs parsley or cilantro, leaves only, chopped
1 tsp toasted sesame seeds

DUMPLINGS
1 lb pkg wonton skins
3/4 lb ground pork
1/4 lb green cabbage
3/4 tsp salt
1 tsp dry sherry
Ground white pepper to taste

Finely chop cabbage and mix with pork, salt, sherry and white pepper. Place 1/2 T pork mixture in middle of each wonton skin. Fold in half and seal edges with water. Put 8 cups water in medium saucepan and bring to boil. Drop in wontons. Cook until they rise to surface (approx. 4 minutes) Take out and drain. Arrange on serving plate, pour sauce over and sprinkle with topping. Makes 30–35 dumplings. (Dumplings can also be fried).
   Kevin Tung, The Golden Plate Restaurant

is in evidence on one shelf, and a startling selection of soup stocks and bases, including Mama Sita's, a brand I've noticed in many Asian stores recently. Here it's a guava soup base, to make the Filipino sour soup called sinigang. They have dried sea cucumbers, black and strange-looking, and lots of sauces and marinades. I can't resist a packet of Robertson's mango jelly powder (Jelly is jello in England). It's quite delicious and very exotic-tasting. I also try some Portuguese sauce, a kind of marinade made with coconut. Well, if you know exactly what to do with it, it isn't an adventure, is it?

Krungthai Market

11700 Montview 343-9450
Daily, 10 am–6 pm.

Phon Techapaikaweekul has a wonderful variety of fresh vegetables when I visit his store. His English is good, and he's very knowledgeable about the different kinds of vegetables he carries. When I'm there, he has fresh durian, baby bananas, white Thai eggplant, chayote, mangoes, jicama and plantains, and 3 or 4 different kinds of basil. His produce is seasonal to some extent, and fresh vegetables and fruit arrive often. Like most of the Thai grocers, Phon has large bags of rice and a selection of Oriental noodles. I also find some wonderfully unusual and sometimes puzzling things like a soup mix labeled, "chicken flavored porridge". It probably means some kind of congee, also occasionally called gruel. Congee is a thick rice soup. Other treasures include small cans of Thai curry–red, yellow and masaman–all quite delicious with meat or shrimp, coconut milk and kaffir lime leaves. Annatto seeds are one of the many spices available here. They can be hard to find, although I'm more familiar with their uses in South American dishes than in Asian ones. By western standards, the shop is rather dark and disorganized, but it contains some wonderful items difficult to find elsewhere. There are many canned soups, including one described as stewed fish maw. You can find galgangal here, the root sometimes described as "Thai ginger". It adds a distinct flavor to curries and other dishes, and it's well worth seeking out the fresh kind, as it's so much better than the dried or powdered.

Laotian Oriental Food Store

7141 Irving, Westminster 428-3694
Daily, 10 am–6:30 pm.

Exotic canned goods, like yanang leaves, banana blossoms, cassia flowers and the more familiar bamboo shoots, are a feature of this friendly Asian market. Canned mushrooms of all descriptions, pickled tamarind and palm sugar, preserved mangoes, coconut milk... the exotic saga continues. A good selection of hot and sweet chile sauces, hoisin, oyster sauces, hot curry pastes and shao hsing–fine rice cooking wine–can be found here. One of the specialties of most Asian markets is the enormous bags of rice, and this store is no exception. There are also lots of noodles of various kinds and banh trang, the rice paper wrappers for egg rolls and such. Fresh vegetables and fruit include green mangoes, cilantro, limes, two kinds of tiny eggplants, garlic, beans, squash and mint. Baskets and bowls, and some wonderfully exotic brooms, are also in evidence. Desserts of various kinds are provided by Pad Thai restaurant, and sit ready to tempt you on your way out. I'm always amazed to find English products like Horlicks, a malted milk drink, in Asian markets, tattered remnants of the days when many Asian countries were colonies. Horlicks is a malted milk bedtime drink. Somehow I can't imagine drinking it after an exotic meal!

Lek's Asian Market

112 Del Mar Circle, Aurora, 366-2429
Monday–Saturday, 10 am–7 pm. Sunday, 10 am–6 pm.
Winter closing 5–6 pm.

Lek's Market is a good place for shoppers who want to begin cooking with Asian ingredients. The store is very clean and bright, and offers a wonderful variety of exotic produce, teas and coffees, canned goods and more! The array of noodles, rice sticks, egg noodles and somen, and other such goods is awesome and there are big bags of rice, and also bulk rice of different kinds available loose, so you can just buy as much or as little as you want. Canned hearts of palm, lotus shoots and all kinds of exotic fruits are always worth a try. I use them for pies and crumbles, but was very surprised once when I opened a can of jackfruit to use in a pie and found I'd bought green jackfruit instead of my usual jackfruit in syrup. The nearest taste to it is artichokes. So I put it into the salad instead of making the pie! Many mixes for Filipino soups and stews can be found here, and other such items, like a tamarind soup mix that's very good, and a Hawaiian-style curry mix that looks intriguing. There's also an instant sour coconut paste for making tom ka gai, the famous Thai chicken soup. Thai curry pastes seem to get more numerous and various, and there are panang and masaman curry as well as the red, green and yellow curries. Lek has many teas and coffees. Thai coffee is often called oliang powder, and it's made with corn and sesame as well as coffee. Jasmine tea and ginger tea are both here, and coffee with chicory, just like you find in New Orleans. Fresh fruits and vegetables are seasonal, and I find fresh durian, a fruit that resembles a spiky pineapple. It has a heavenly taste, but a hellish smell, so bad that it's been banned on some airlines. Red chilis, kaffir lime leaves, indispensible for Thai curries, small bananas, Thai eggplant and daikon–they're all here. Exotic drinks include coconut nectar, pennywort, tamarind juice and mango drink. Lek is very helpful with recipes and suggestions about how to use the ingredients you can find here. She also sometimes has a cookbook, in English and in Thai, that gives instructions on making Thai dishes in American kitchens. It's very helpful, and the recipes I've made from it have turned out wonderful!

Little Saigon Supermarket

375 S. Federal 937-8860
Daily, 9 am – 9 pm.

Little Saigon has undergone a facelift along with its change of name and ownership. It's much more open inside, and each aisle is neatly marked with signs designating contents in Vietnamese and English. This is a real boon to the novice ethnic shopper. There's an aisle of Filipino food, including the ubiquitous Mama Sita's mixes: this time for kare kare (oxtail stew) and menudo or afritada as perhaps it's called in the Philippines. There's also Filipino yam jam. On the end of one aisle is a rack of small cake molds, several of which are made in Sweden. How do they fit in? There are lots of teas, including instant ginger and another that's labeled interestingly but not very helpfully "thirst-quenching tea". As well as coconut milk, there is powdered coconut cream powder. Canned palm juice, longan drink and chrysanthemum tea are all available in cans in the refrigerator case. But what are pickled lemons doing here? I thought they were part of Middle Eastern cuisine. And then there are cans of something called pickled hog plums. They sound interesting, but I pass in favor of the fresh vegetables and fruits like green papaya and baby bananas.

Mekong

1076 S. Federal, 937-7271
Daily, 9 am–8 pm.

Most of the Asian markets in town have some ready-to-eat food for takeout, usually near the door when you go in. Mekong has a much more extensive deli section, with Vietnamese submarine sandwiches (if you've never tried these, you must–they're delicious and very inexpensive. Here they're $1.50 or so.), barbecue pork dumplings, shrimp dumplings and other Asian deli foods. There's also a fine variety of che, the Asian drink/dessert that's made with layers of sweet mung beans, agar agar (a gelatin made from seaweed) and sometimes coconut, all layered with ice. These are a little foreign for American tastes, but quite well-flavored and interesting. Mekong has a great selection of noodles, as well as meats, soy sauces and vinegars, nuoc mam (Vietnamese fish sauce) and homemade tofu. The people here are very helpful and go out of their way to help me with a recipe.

Midopa Market

10700 E. Iliff, Aurora 695-4803
Monday–Saturday, 9 am–9 pm. Closed Sunday.

Fresh vegetables here include four different kinds of hot peppers, two kinds of pickling cucumbers and several kinds of mushrooms, including shimeji (oyster mushrooms), and enoki. There's a wealth of tofu, huge jars of kim chee and equally huge bags of peeled garlic. The many varieties of beans include dried soybeans, peeled mung beans, black beans and brown beans (which are chick peas). There are several kinds of rice, too, including glutinous rice and wild glutinous rice. Sauces include soy sauces, mustard and miso, bulgogi and tempura sauces and different sauces for shabu shabu, a Japanese-style meat fondue. You'll find rice wines and vinegars, pickled daikon and salted shrimp, and many kinds of flour and starch, including barley flour, wheat flour, mung bean, corn and potato starch. There are many kinds of noodles and sheets of dried seaweed and yakinori. As usual in Asian markets, there are many kinds of crackers, cookies and candies, the most intriguing of which is a bag of plastic mini cups about the size of the cups of cream that come with coffee in some restaurants. They have a fruit drink inside.

ASIAN INGREDIENTS

Agar agar: *A gelatin made from seaweed. Used instead of gelatin in hot countries because it doesn't need to be cool to gel.*

Bean Curd or Tofu: *A cream-colored gel made from dried soybeans. Dried soybeans are soaked, puréed and boiled in water. The liquid is strained and mixed with a coagulant or solidifier which makes it form curds. These are compressed into bean curd.*

Coconut Milk: *In many Asian countries, milk and cheese are not used at all, so coconut milk replaces them in desserts, is used to make cooling drinks and to cool the hot spices used in curries. Coconut milk tends to curdle if it is overcooked, so add it towards the end of cooking and stir with a ladle, lifting and pouring the milk to prevent boiling.*

Fish Sauce, Nuoc Mam: *A strongly flavored, pungent sauce used in Southeast Asia in much the same way as soy sauce in China*

Galangal or Thai ginger: *This spice has a hot peppery taste that could be described as a cross between horseradish and ginger. It's used in hot chili sauces and Thai curries. Known in Europe as galingale, it was long thought to be an aphrodisiac.*

Lemon Grass: *A major ingredient in Thai, Indonesian and Malaysian cooking, lemon grass is a fragrant grass with a white bulb and long, green leaves. It can be used by chopping the white part finely or crushing the whole plant to release the lemon flavor and taking it out of the dish before serving.*

Sambals: *Malaysian or Indonesian side dishes served with meals to complement flavors. Often spicy, they can be raw or cooked.*

Satay: *Indonesian, Thai or Malaysian dish of skewered seasoned meat, poultry or seafood grilled over charcoal and served with a dipping sauce. Sauces can be made with peanuts or sweet soy.*

Sichuan peppercorns: *These are not true peppercorns, but the aromatic red-brown seeds of the prickly ash tree. They have a peppery, lemon flavor.*

Tamarind: *Fruit of the tamarind tree found in India, Indonesia and Malaysia, tamarind has a distinct, sweet-tart flavor. Used in curries, braised dishes and sauces to give a sharp flavor.*

Oriental Food Market

1750-84 30th Street, Boulder 442-7830
Monday–Friday, 10 am–7 pm; Saturday, 10 am–6 pm;
Sunday, noon–4 pm.

Noodles of all kinds line the shelves in this Boulder market, from corn and rice sticks to Korean buckwheat noodles. Many instant soups look interesting too–egg flower, seaweed and miso are the most readily recognizable. There are many Indonesian ingredients, as well as Korean kim chee mix and Chinese barbecue sauce. Patak Indian pastes and pickles are next to different kinds of curry powder, and papads to be puffed up to accompany tasty Indian dips. Several varieties of dal are piled up here as well. Vinegars of all kinds, and oils like mustard and almond oil and even chili oil offer many choices for the ethnic cook. Galangal or Thai ginger is in the freezer, chilling with kaffir lime leaves and lemon grass.

NUOC CHAM
Vietnamese Dipping Sauce

1 cup nuoc mam (fish sauce)
2 Tbsp hoisin sauce
3 Tbsp rice vinegar
2–3 cloves garlic, crushed
1 tsp hot crushed chile pepper
1/4 cup Coco Rico coconut soda
2 Tbsp crushed unsalted peanuts

Mix all ingredients together and thicken if necessary with a little tapioca flour. Serve with Vietnamese spring rolls or other Vietnamese dishes.   –Thao Le, Mekong Market

GOI CUON–SPRING ROLLS

Rice papers, Lettuce leaves.

Filling: 5 large shrimp, chopped; 3/4 cup fresh bean sprouts, 1 carrot, shredded, 1/2 cup each mint and cilantro leaves; 1/2 cup cooked, chopped pork loin. Mix filling ingredients. Soften rice papers in hot water. Put 1/2 lettuce leaf on rice paper. On lettuce, put 1–2 T filling mixture. Roll up in rice paper, folding ends inside. Work with only 2 sheets rice paper at a time, covering the rest of the package with a wet towel. Serve with nuoc cham.

Oriental Grocery Store

7301 Federal, Westminster 430-4582
Daily, 9 am – 8 pm.

Fresh herbs and vegetables are available here, bagged in the cooler: mint, peppers, basil and others. There's an abundance of fish sauce and chili sauce, as well as whole grain soy sauce. Big bags of rice are stacked up, and noodles and spring roll skins are well represented. There are many small tins of Thai curry: red, green, masaman and others. There are also many kinds of canned mushrooms, including straw and oyster mushrooms. Korean barbecue mix is familiar, as are the bamboo shoots in brine, but what on earth is pickled jujube? To my great surprise, I find they are red dates, well-known in China where several different kinds are cultivated. They can be sweet or sour. Thai coffee and several different kinds of tea, such as jasmine and green tea, can be purchased here, and chocolate cream wafers to eat with them.

Oriental Market

1443 Chester, Aurora 366-0454
Monday–Saturday, 9 am – 8 pm. Closed Sunday.

Ginseng drinks, a well as another "refreshing Chinese herb drink" are on the shelves here not far from all the different kinds of tea, including green, ginseng and jasmine. There are all kinds, sizes and descriptions of dried noodles, as well as udon noodles in soup base. Oyster sauce, hot chili sauce, fish sauce and hoisin sauce are abundant here, as are sesame oil, soy and tamari sauces and sauces for Korean dishes like bulgogi, and Japanese tempura, shabu shabu, sukiyaki and tonkatsu. This last is a deep-fried pork cutlet, served over shredded cabbage with a thin, Worcestershire sauce based dressing. Bulk spices, soy beans, red beans and hot pepper are here, as well as kimchi, lots of different kinds of frozen fish, quail eggs in brine, three kinds of millet, mung beans and sesame seeds. Fresh vegetables include napa cabbage, fresh burdock root, radishes, bean sprouts, chiles and fresh ginger and garlic. There are Asian pears and big bags of pine nuts. Canned fish like eels, squid, cuttlefish and mackerel are here, as well as dumpling wrappers, gyoza and wonton skins, and Korean-style cakes and cookies.

Pacific Mercantile

1925 Lawrence   295-0293
Monday–Saturday, 8 am–6 pm; Sunday, 9 am–2 pm.

Walking into Pacific Mercantile, I am struck by the freshness and variety of their vegetables: bok choy, bitter melon, daikon, taro root, gobo (this last is known as burdock in English, and is eaten cooked or made into pickles.) There are also several kinds of fresh mushrooms, including shiitake, enoki and shimeji. The fish is also fresh and quite a variety is offered: tuna, snapper, scallops, shrimp, sea bass, mackerel, mussels and octopus, to name a few. Quails' eggs are in the same refrigerator case; they're used for sushi. There are many kinds of Japanese noodles, both in the refrigerator case and dried. They include udon noodles, thick white wheat noodles served either cold or in soup, chuka soba and the dish these thick ramen noodles are used to make, which is yaki soba. I counted 20 different kinds of green tea, but there are probably more. The Japanese usually drink only green tea. However, in the Chinese food section, with the shark's fin and winter melon soup, there's oolong and jasmine tea as well. There's also a good selection of Indonesian food, including sambals, ketcap manis, which is the Indonesian soy sauce, and mixes for Indonesian peanut sauce. Many kinds of rice are available in large bags: sweet rice, brown rice and others. Bulk spices are also available. Some of the most unusual are lily flower and Szechuan peppers.

Pacific Ocean Marketplace

2200 W. Alameda, #2-B 936-4845 Fax: 936-2336
Daily, 9 am – 8 pm.

If you're looking for chicken feet, make tracks for Pacific Ocean Marketplace. They also have live crabs and lobsters, and their shrimp are pretty inexpensive. The wall of value you see when you walk in has mostly noodles, but there's a considerable number of different kinds. Tofu in abundance and in various forms can be found here, along with dumpling wrappers and mixes for miso and egg flower soup. Hot pepper abounds, both white and red, and Chinese sweet and sour mix and sweet and sour spareribs too. Korean barbecue mix vies with Philippine adobo mix, and satay sauces, satay pastes, hot chili sauces and sambals look equally enticing.

Pickled limes and palm sugar can be found, as well as a lot of canned tropical fruit like longans, lychees and jackfruit. Fresh vegetables include okra, long beans, eggplants, taro and cassava root. Signs are in English as well as Asian languages, which makes it easier for Americans to shop here. There are lots of dishes, woks and other housewares. At first I was surprised to find cruller mix, but there are Indonesian specialties here, and the word cruller is originally Dutch. (The Dutch colonized Indonesia). Maybe crullers would be good with the adjacent sweet coconut spread. Come here, too, for banana leaves for wrapping different kinds of food.

Seoul Oriental Market

6150 N. Federal 650-0101
Monday – Saturday, 9 am – 8 pm. Closed Sunday.

Slow down as you drive on Federal, or you'll drive right by this Korean market, run by Mr. Chang Kung O and his wife Kyong O. It's hidden behind a car wash on the east side of the street, and the only sign leads to a nursery that's round the back. However, once you find it, there's a wealth of Asian ingredients inside. Enormous jars of kim chee (kimchi), a hot and spicy fermented pickle, made most often from napa cabbage, but sometimes from other vegetables like radish or green onion, and seasoned with chiles, salt and garlic, dominate the refrigerator case. There's also a ton of hot bean paste and black bean paste. I find many different kinds of tea, some familiar, like Darjeeling, oolong, jasmine and green tea, and some less so, such as roasted barley tea. I've tried this in

Korean restaurants, and it's an acquired taste. Noodles of all kinds abound, including soba noodles and various kinds of vermicelli. Hot pepper pastes and Korean barbecue sauce can also be found here. There are fresh garlic and ginger and many kinds of Golden Curry Mix, not just hot, medium and mild, but pastes as well as powders. Soups, or gruels as they are sometimes described, raise expectations of Oliver Twist, but they just mean thick kinds of soups like sweet red bean and pumpkin. Sweets and candies are amazing in their variations. Black Touch chewy chocolate and breath freshener beads with their own plastic dispenser are two of the most interesting-looking.

Tan Phat Oriental Market

1001 S. Federal 935-3766
Daily, 9 am – 7 pm.

Tan Phat is a good place to go if you're just beginning to venture into Asian markets. The people here are very helpful and friendly and there's usually someone who speaks pretty good English. They also have many of the major fresh ingredients you need for Thai cooking. You can find sweet basil here, as well as galangal. Sometimes called Thai ginger, it doesn't actually taste like ginger, though it is very pungent. You can also find fresh mint and lemon grass, as well as Thai eggplants, small, green, beautiful-looking vegetables often used in Thai curries. There are lots of sambals, chili sauces and soy sauce, rice vinegars and fish sauce. Fresh fish is also available here. I always enjoy seeing the colorful Thai shrines and statues they have for sale.

MASAMAN CURRY

SPICES:
9 Anaheim chiles, peeled and seeded
1 Tbsp coriander seeds
3 dollar size slices galangal (Thai ginger)
1 tsp cumin seeds
3 Tbsp sliced lemon grass
1/5 whole nutmeg, grated
Same amt cinnamon, grated
1 Tbsp cilantro stems, chopped
7 shallots, chopped
12 whole white peppercorns
5 whole cloves
1 Tbsp shrimp paste
5 white cardamom seeds

Roast spices in a hot pan until aromatic. When cool, put in blender with 1 can coconut milk. Cook gently (do not boil) until it smells good. Set aside.

2 lbs chicken, boned, skinned and cut into 2" pieces
3 cans coconut milk
1 cup roasted peanuts
3 potatoes, peeled and cut into 2" pieces
12 pearl onions
1/2 cup fish sauce
1/2 cup coconut sugar
1/2 cup tamarind juice
3 Tbsp lime juice

Cook the above ingredients on low heat (do not boil) until chicken and potatoes are almost cooked. Add spice mixture and cook gently for about 1/2 hour. Serve over rice.
Jit Na-Bangchang, J's Noodles Restaurant

CHINESE STEAMED GARLIC CUSTARD

   4 eggs
   2 cups chicken broth
   1/2 cup green chiles, roasted, peeled, seeded, chopped into 1" dice
   1/4 cup toasted garlic
   1/2 lb cooked sausage (optional)

Mix eggs and broth together gently. Do not beat. Add garlic and green chile pieces. Pour into oiled casserole dish. Top with sliced sausage if desired. Set up wok as steamer. Cover casserole with foil and steam in wok. Cook until egg is just set. Time will vary widely, depending on the dish, but averages about 20 minutes. Serves 4
                            Sam Arnold, The Fort Restaurant

Xuan Trang

1095 S. Federal 936-7537
Daily, 8:30 am – 7:30 pm.

This market doesn't just have foodstuffs. There are a lot of household goods as well. Candles, china, pots and teapots, soup spoons and chopsticks, big trays like they use for the injera bread at Ethiopian restaurants and bright colored bowls and colanders in every imaginable size. You can even find shoes and purses here, and there are often several eager buyers trying on shoes in the middle of the canned fruit department! The selection of vegetables is good, with baby bok choy, okra and taro root, to name just a few. Sauces abound, like black bean garlic sauce, Malaysian curry powder and hoisin, as well as the usual soy and chili sauces and the less usual kimchi, sweet and sour, Chinese barbecue and Japanese teriyaki. Soup bases for Filipino sinigang and tamarind soups are here, cheek by jowl with Hale's syrups, in mundane cream soda and exotic mali (jasmine) flavors. Here I also find fresh betel leaves, used in Asian cooking to wrap meat, but I've had them in England, in Indian restaurants, wrapped around after-dinner spices, topped with gold or silver filigree–the elusive paan. I'm very excited; even though they're $12 a pound, that works out to less than 20 cents each.

British Markets

Canos Collection

235 Fillmore 322-0654
Monday–Saturday, 10:30 am–5:30 pm. Closed Sunday.

This pretty little store is inside an arcade, on a balcony overlooking the atrium. Scones and Welsh cakes are available here for $7.50 a dozen, You can also get crumpets, Devon cream and British bangers (sausages)–the kind that go with mash. Joyce, the soft-spoken Welsh woman who runs Canos Collection, makes shepherd's pie for lunch sometimes, and has added chicken pot pie to the menu. If you're lucky, rhubarb crumble or trifle may be on the lunch or tea menu, and, of course, tea is served from 11 am to 5 pm. Joyce is thinking of adding finger sandwiches to the tea menu, to be served with scones. Don't confuse cream tea with high tea, by the way. Cream tea includes scones and clotted cream; high tea is more of a full meal with meat or cheese and much more substantial than other forms of tea!

The English Teacup

1930 S. Havana, Aurora 751-3032
Monday–Saturday, 10 am–5:30 pm. Closed Sunday.

Jeanne Fox, the owner of this elegant little shop, has many souvenirs of England, and a lovely collection of English tea pots, china, Toby jugs and other Anglophilia for sale. Teas include Typhoo and PG Tips, and digestive biscuits and shortbread to go with it. Cold drinks like Ribena, a blackcurrant concentrate, squash, another concentrate, usually orange or lemon, to which you add water, hot or cold, and lemon barley water, which I always associate with comfort during illnesses, since my mother always made a jug of it if we were sick as kids.

Jeanne's collection of jams, preserves and marmalades is jolly good, and includes lemon curd, all kinds of marmalade, including Lemon Shred and Orange Shred (with thinly sliced peel) and many more too numerous to mention. Trifle and custard mixes make tempting desserts in very little time, and a blackcurrant cheesecake mix would make a nice change from the usual American kinds. Steak and kidney pies, Yorkshire pudding mixes and a mix for treacle pudding are all reminders of cold winter days when we need something to stick to our ribs and keep out the damp and the fog. Oxo and bisto probably aren't familiar to most, but they're bouillon-like additions to gravies and sauces. Soups like oxtail and mulligatawny (this last is a curried chicken soup) are hearty and flavorful. Don't forget the malt vinegar–how would any self-respecting English person eat their fish and chips without it?

KINDS OF TEA

There are three basic kinds of tea: black tea, which includes almost all Indian tea, green tea, which includes almost all Japanese tea, and oolong, which has some of the characteristics of each.

Black tea: *is dried, rolled to bruise the leaves and release the flavor and fermented to develop the fragrance of the leaves. The fermentation is then stopped by firing–exposing the tea to a blast of hot, dry air. Examples: English breakfast, Darjeeling, Lapsang Souchong.*

Green tea: *is not fermented, but is steamed, rolled and fired. The leaves remain green. It has a milder flavor than black tea, and is the tea of choice in Asia. Examples: gunpowder, basket fried.*

Oolong: *is partially fermented tea. It is sometimes mixed with jasmine or gardenia to make a scented tea*

Specialty teas: *These teas are often flavored with spices or herbs to make flavored teas.*

Herb teas: *Also known as tisanes, these teas are made from infusions of herbs, flowers and spices, and contain no true tea leaves. .*

House of Windsor

1050 S. Wadsworth, Lakewood 936-9029
Monday–Friday, 10 am–5 pm; Saturday, 10 am–4 pm.
Closed Sunday.

If you're looking for authentic British hospitality, the House of Windsor is a very attractive version of a British tearoom, with a lovely assortment of china and British food products as well. Brenda and Derek Williams are the creators of this little island of civility in a shopping center at Wadsworth and Mississippi, with its tables for tea and air of graciousness. I take people here for business meetings in the mornings sometimes, because it's so nice and quiet, and you can sit and indulge in a pot of tea and one or two of their lovely pastries, like hazelnut torte or lemon meringue pie, or a scone with jam and cream. The House of Windsor has its own private label preserves, in several flavors, such as raspberry, apricot, blackberry, apricot orange and strawberry orange. Brenda has also developed her own scone mix, or you can buy them ready-made to take home. Pork pies, pasties, sausage rolls–all can be purchased to eat there or take away. Pies and cakes are also available whole or by the slice. And for those hankering for imported British products, look for Branston pickle, a kind of chutney, or picalilli, a highly seasoned vegetable relish. To drink there's Horlicks or Camp coffee, a bottled coffee with chicory. Also, if you want an entire tea party to go, the House of Windsor will cater your party or event. Wouldn't it be luverly?

The Lemon Cheese Company

2545 Youngfield, Golden 237-6678
Monday–Friday, 10 am–5:30 pm; Saturday, 10 am–4 pm.

If you're looking for a little Turkish delight, or a little of any other kind of delight, The Lemon Cheese Company would be a good place to start. There are lots of mustards and sauces, little jars of preserves, little plum puddings... it's a kind of Lilliput of delights. Turkish delight is a candy made with rosewater and almonds. The taste is delicate and delicious. Just as tasty is the lemon cheese for which this store is named–and you can buy scones to spread it on. Lemon cheese is very similar to lemon curd (that helps, doesn't it?). It's a very creamy, jam-like lemon spread, delicious on scones or toast or even just on a spoon! Of course, the Lemon Cheese Company also has lots of teas: Earl Grey, raspberry, and even the rather un-British apple, mango and blueberry. You can even buy china teapots and tea sets in which to make and serve the tea. If you prefer coffee, there are Kaffeeklatch brand dessert coffees, very prettily packaged, in flavors like coconut rum and caramel. Jams like blackcurrant preserve with armagnac and Elizabethan thin-cut orange marmalade are bursting with fruit flavor. This is a great place to find gifts, or put together a gift basket of interesting foods and other goodies.

Filipino Markets

Nipa Hut

11385 E. Colfax, Aurora 367-1800 Fax: 367-1829
Tuesday–Sunday, 10 am–9 pm. Closed Monday.

The Nipa Hut describes itself as the home of the finest Filipino cuisine. Since the restaurant has opened, Gil and Rita Asunçion, the owners, have added a small market in the back of the store, carrying Filipino food items. Don't expect to go home and make all the wonderful dishes they have in the restaurant, but do try some of the specialty ingredients you can find here. Mama Sita's mixes and sauces figure large (you'll see what I mean when you look at the picture of Mama Sita) in the repertoire of products. There's chicken in adobo sauce, among others, and you can also find banana sauce, which is a much more wonderful substitute for ketchup, and other delicious sauces. Check out the purple yam powder, used to make yam jam, the fish sauce, salted anchovies and sweet macapuño balls, made with coconut. There's also annatto, that elusive orange seed, and coconut milk, as well as, surprisingly, cans of Nestlé's thick cream. If you haven't tried this cream, serve it with scones and strawberry jam or to top scones, fruit or trifle. I'm not sure how it fits into Filipino cooking, although I know it would make a dynamite topping for leche flan, the rich and delicious Filipino version of flan that they serve here in the restaurant.

LEMON CURD
–It tastes better than it sounds

Lemon curd is made from lemon juice, sugar, butter and eggs. These ingredients are cooked in a double boiler and strained, and produce a creamy, delicious spread for bread, scones or as a filling for tarts or pies. It's incredibly good spread on scones and topped with whipped cream. You can find canned whipped cream in many ethnic markets, including Middle Eastern and some Asian markets. Lemon curd originated in Britain, and is available in jars at many gourmet shops. The lemon cheese at the Lemon Cheese Company is a variation on this product. A quick and easy lemon curd mix is available from Great British Tastes. Call them at 526-1166. They also have an orange curd mix, scone mix and an Irish soda bread mix. They're all jolly good, too.

German Markets

Black Forest Specialties

9436 W. 58th, Arvada 425-0265
Tuesday–Friday, 9 am–5:30 pm; Saturday, 9 am–3 pm.
Closed Sunday & Monday.

Although Ingrid swears everything is exactly the same as it used to be, I detect some subtle changes over the last couple of years. She still has the same German specialties, but the deli foods seem to have increased. There's Brie, Camembert, a nice selection of ham and sausage, head cheese, as well as several kinds of mustards, herbal teas and, of course, pickles and sauerkraut. Syrups like blackcurrant, strawberry and raspberry edge up to mixes for sauerbraten and goulash, and a farina dumpling mix. Ingrid's customers are from many different parts of Europe, including Germany, Hungary, Czechoslovakia and Poland. Black Forest Specialties is hidden in a shopping center, and can't be seen from the street, so you might have to drive around a bit to find it.

GLACE

3 potatoes
1 cup flour
1 egg
1/2 tsp baking powder
1/2 tsp salt
1/4 cup milk or more to make soft dough
1 cup warm half and half
1/2 stick butter
2 slices white bread

Peel and slice potatoes. Boil in salted water until almost done. Mix next 5 ingredients together and drop by teaspoons into water with potatoes. Cook till done, about 10 minutes. Drain well and place in bowl. Melt butter in frying pan. Add white bread torn into pieces. Cook till browned. Pour butter and bread over potatoes and glace. Then pour half and half over the top. Serve.
Tammi Davis, Divine Temptations
(This is an old German recipe handed down from Tammi's great-grandmother.)

Indian Markets

Bombay Bazaar

3140 South Parker Road, Aurora   369-1010
Tuesday, 4–8:30 pm; Wednesday–Monday, 11 am–8:30 pm.

Nami Bagga and his wife Neetu now own this store, and they have made it much cleaner, more open and much more appealing. They also appear to keep more predictable hours, which is a blessing if you have to travel far to get here. Almonds, cashews and green cardamoms are here, together with many kinds of tea. A fine selection of curry pastes, chutneys and pickles line the shelves, together with many kinds of dal (pulses) in a multitude of colors: yellow, peach and green, as well as a variety of mixed black and white urid dal. Don't miss the masalas (spice mixtures) for chicken and chana; the chappati flour, or jaggery, a kind of coarse, unrefined sugar with a sweet, wine-like smell and flavor. Jaggery is sometimes the same as palm sugar, but not in Indian stores, where palm sugar is called gur. Try some of the Indian food mixes, like chicken tikka, idli or kofta curry, and don't miss the samosas (ready-to-eat triangular pastries filled with vegetables or meat or a combination of both). Best of all, if you're an ice cream lover, is the exotic ice cream, in which the choices are often either pistachio or mango. They're wonderful.

TANDOOR

A tandoor is a clay oven, shaped rather like a beehive with an opening in the top for putting the food in. Indian breads like naan can be stuck to the side of the tandoor and allowed to cook there. Tandoori chicken and sometimes fish are cooked in this oven, which has no temperature controls but which cooks whole pieces of chicken or fish or various kinds of kebabs beautifully by quickly searing the outside while leaving the interior moist. Tandoori spices can be bought to make the tandoori chicken that is so often found in Indian and Pakistani restaurants. Don't worry if your chicken isn't quite as orange as the chicken you eat in Indian restaurants. Theirs is often colored with an orange-red food coloring that's added to the chicken as it marinates. Since most of us don't have a tandoor at home, we have to improvise, but I've found that quite respectable tandoori meat and fish can be made on the outdoor barbecue.

INDIAN INGREDIENTS

Basmati: Fragrant, expensive rice grown in the Dehradun region of India

Besan: Chickpea flour

Biryani: Festive dish made with rice and spiced meat or chicken

Chana: Chickpea (chana dal is a split chickpea pulse)

Chai: Spiced Indian tea

Chapati: Flat bread made with whole wheat flour

Dal: Pulse, lentil

Dhosa: Pancake of rice and legumes

Garam: Hot (garam marsala are hot spices)

Idli: Southern Indian steamed rice and lentil cake

Kofta: Meatball

Korma: Rich meat dish

Kulfi: Indian "ice cream" often flavored with mango or pistachio

Lassi: Indian drink made with ice and yogurt, and fruit or salt

Masala: A mixture of spices used in Indian cooking. They are made by grinding whole spices into powder.

Pan (paan): Betel leaf; a collection of spices wrapped in a betel leaf and served after an Indian meal. These can be very elaborate, sometimes containing gold or silver leaf called vark.

Papad or pappadum: A wafer-like cracker or bread made from lentil, rice or potato flour. They are deep-fried and served as a snack, sometimes with chutneys.

Paratha: Layered, buttery Indian bread

Poori: Deep-fried Indian bread

Raita: Indian side dish made with yoghurt and a vegetable, often cucumber

Samosas: Pastries stuffed with meat and vegetables and deep-fried

Tajmahal Imports

3095-C S. Peoria, Aurora 751-8571
Daily, 11 am – 8 pm. Closed Tuesday.

At Tajmahal you can find all the wonderful spicy condiments, chutneys and other exotic ingredients you need to make tasty and delicious Indian food. The store carries Indian tea, together with tea masala – the special spices you need to make spicy, smooth Indian tea or chai. There's also a great selection of Indian snack foods and many kinds of dal – split peas, lentils, garbanzos (chana dal). The red lentils (actually, they're a beautiful salmon color) are sometimes hard to find in regular markets. The selection of Indian breads is also very good. They have poori, chapati, and naan in the refrigerator case and pappadums in packages. Pappadums are made from lentil flour. They look like a cross between a tortilla and a flat bread, but when cooked in hot oil they puff up and taste delicious. You can also heat them in the microwave. Tajmahal has a selection of Indian spices, including aromatic green cardamom seeds, and many different kinds of flour, like gram flour and moong dal flour, and even urad bean flour, which is used to make pappadums. Best of all, in the refrigerator case at the front of the shop is a selection of desserts, most of them milk-based and tasting rather like very rich and fabulous fudge. Some are flour-based and taste more like halvah. Also, to my delight, there are samosas, one of the many Indian snacks you can buy from street vendors on the streets in most Indian cities – and in parts of London – just waiting to be taken home and crisped in the oven!

Tejal International Foods

10351 Grant St. Thornton 450-4164
Wednesday – Monday, 11 am – 8 pm. Closed Tuesday.

If you're looking for prepared Indian foods, either in the refrigerator case or in cans, Tejal is the place to find them. They have many foods, especially vegetarian dishes, that just need to be heated, like sag or palak paneer: greens or spinach with Indian cheese. There's also a fine variety of mixes, so you can make your own idlis or dhosas, and other dishes. Idlis are steamed rice or lentil cakes from the southern part of India, and dhosas are rice and lentil pancakes. Tejal also offers many kinds of dal and pulses, whole, split and ground into flour, a wide variety of spices and many kinds of chat and other Indian snacks. Pappadums, thin wafers made of lentil flour that puff when fried, come in several different flavors, and there are many kinds of chutney and pickles. To drink, try one of their tropical flavored mango or guava drinks, or a ginger beer. There's also a selection of teas. Tropical ice creams and kulfis are some of the most delightful to be found anywhere. Kulfi is an Indian ice cream made of boiled-down milk solids. For me, the most exciting find is that they not only have paan masala–the mixture of spices to make the paan that Indians eat after a meal–but also the fresh betel leaf to wrap them in. On weekends, you can buy the paan ready-made for $1 each. They're an experience.

CHANA BHATURA
Spicy Garbanzo Beans

1 cup chopped onions
1/2 cup cooked, diced potatoes
1/2 cup chopped tomatoes
1-1/2 cups water
16 oz can garbanzo beans

SPICES

1 tsp fresh minced garlic
1 tsp salt
1 Tbsp vegetable oil
1/4 tsp turmeric
1/2 tsp pure red chili powder
2 tsp dhanajeer (1/2 tsp cumin powder + 1-1/2 tsp. coriander powder)
1/2 tsp garam masala or "chana masala"
1/2 tsp lemon juice (if needed)
2 tsp fresh chopped cilantro (optional)

Heat oil, add onions and sauté on medium low for 5 mins. Add garlic, sauté for 2 mins. Add tomatoes, cover and cook for 5 min. or until well done. Add spices and garam masala. Sauté 1 min. Add 1/4 cup water, cover and cook 3–5 mins. Discard liquid from garbanzo beans and rinse. Add diced potatoes, beans and the rest of the water. Bring to a boil and simmer uncovered 10 mins. Add lemon juice if needed, and cilantro. Serve hot with tortillas or Indian bread.
    Jessica Shah, Mij Bani Indian Restaurant, Boulder

Italian Markets

Cosolo's Italian Market

8000 E. Quincy 290-8950
Monday–Friday, 10 am–6 pm; Saturday, 9 am–6 pm. Closed Sunday.

Shirley and Jean run this most attractive and innovative market in the Goldsmith Shopping Center on Quincy near Yosemite. They have homemade pastas, including some flavored with basil or garlic and parsley. At Cosolo's, Tuesday is spaghetti day, and you can get a pound of fresh spaghetti, a pint of marinara sauce and a loaf of garlic bread, serving four, for $4.50. They make their own sausage, both hot and mild Italian, and have meats like pepperoni, capicola and pancetta; cheeses like Gorgonzola, fontina and Parmesan Reggianito, and several kinds of olives as well as caponata, antipasto salad, and my favorite, muffaletta olive salad. Gnocchi, ravioli, fresh rigatoni and tortellini grace the refrigerator case, as well as lasagne, baked ziti and jumbo shells stuffed with spinach and cheese. Olive oils, antipasto and giardiniera, many varieties of dried pasta and jars of baba au rhum are on the shelves, together with cans of whole chestnuts and chestnut spread. Cosolo's pizza kit is legendary, containing sauce, dough and cheese for only $5.50. If you don't have an Italian mama to cook for you, go to Cosolo's!

ITALIAN BARBEQUE SAUCE

- 1 small onion, diced
- 1 Tbsp olive oil
- 2 Tbsp minced fresh garlic
- 1 can tomatoes, crushed
- 1/4 cup brown sugar
- 1/4 cup balsamic vinegar
- 1 Tbsp mixed fresh chopped herbs: basil, thyme, sage, rosemary, oregano
- 1/4 tsp each salt & pepper

In a small saucepan, sauté onion until transparent. Add garlic and sauté about 2 minutes. Add herbs and vinegar, then sugar, and boil 2 more minutes. Add tomatoes and simmer very slowly until thick. Add salt and pepper. Use as a sauce for pizza crust or on chicken or beef for grilling.

          Phil Jones, Rosso's Ristorante, Red Lion Hotel

Spinelli's Market

4621 E. 23rd Avenue (23rd & Dexter)   329-8143
Monday–Friday, 9 am–7 pm. Saturday, 8 am–6 pm.
Closed Sunday.

They have lots of fresh produce, including Colorado plums and peaches, in this little neighborhood market. However, there are also quite a lot of Italian products. "I guess the Italian stuff just got away from us," says Jerry Spinelli, who owns the store with his wife, Mary Ellen. Olive oils, balsamic vinegar, Italian pasta sauce, mascarpone and mozzarella, pizza dough, Italian sausage, and a slew of different kinds of noodles–well, after all, Jerry has Italian blood, and so he couldn't resist adding an Italian touch to this very nice neighborhood shop. You'll also find bread, teas and coffee beans and, of course, amaretti cookies. If you haven't tried these crisp, airy macaroons made with bitter almond paste, you're in for a real treat! Get them at Spinelli's.

Vinnola's Market

7750 W. 38th Avenue, Wheat Ridge   421-3955
Monday–Friday, 9 am–6 pm; Saturday, 9 am–5:30 pm.
Closed Sunday.

Vinnola's is one of the best-stocked Italian markets you'll find. They have lots of olive oils, including one in a beautiful little ceramic bottle; balsamic vinegar, superior Italian canned tomatoes and peppers and many varieties of pasta, such as Mama Gina, Sclafani and de Cecco. There's a helpful attitude here that's always appreciated: one woman who only wanted a small amount of sweet peppers was offered a half a jar "I can always use the rest in sandwiches". What an offer! The refrigerator case beckons, with marinara sauce, cheese ravioli, tortellini, and Vinnola's own lasagne. Imported cheeses include Parmigiano Reggiano, provolone, scamorze, Gorgonzola and ricotta. There's sweet mild and sweet hot sausage, and squid, cleaned and uncleaned, is available frozen. Vinnola's is also a bakery, with fresh bread at very reasonable prices, and a number of cookies and other sweet things. A spacious seating area provides a place to sit and enjoy a sandwich or other refreshment.

OLIVE OIL

Olive oil is believed to have originated in the Mediterranean. Olives now grow not only in Spain, Portugal, Italy, France, Greece, Syria, Turkey and Israel, but also in Australia, Africa, California, New Zealand and South America. Olive oil should be stored in a cool, dark place. Storing it in the refrigerator is fine. It may solidify, but will liquefy again at room temperature.

Extra virgin: Made from the first pressing of the olives. The best olive oil is cold-pressed. Intense flavor and aroma. Best for salads, and tossing with vegetables and pasta.

Virgin: Can be from first or second pressing. Good for salads, for marinating meat, fish or vegetables.

Pure olive oil: Previously pressed olives are processed with solvents. The oil may be chemically refined. Good for cooking.

Fine olive oil: Extracted from a mixture of olive pulp and water. Good for cooking.

SHRIMP AMATRICIANA

1 medium onion, diced
2 Tbsp butter
3 Tbsp olive oil
1 lb medium shrimp, peeled & deveined
1 cup pancetta, diced
1 Tbsp garlic, minced
2 cups canned plum tomatoes, cut in strips
Salt & black pepper, to taste
4 Tbsp freshly grated Parmesan
1/4 tsp crushed red pepper
1 lb medium shell pasta

Cook the onion in a saucepan over medium high heat with the butter and olive oil until transparent. Add shrimp and sauté for 2 or 3 minutes till opaque. Remove the shrimp from the saucepan. Add the pancetta and cook over medium heat until crisp. Add the garlic, tomatoes, crushed red pepper and cook approximately 20 minutes. Return shrimp to the sauce. Season with salt and pepper. Toss with the pasta and grated cheese.

Tom Mirabito

Kosher Markets

Utica Grocery

4500 W. Colfax 534-2253
Monday, 9 am–6 pm; Tuesday & Wednesday, 10 am–6 pm;
Thursday, 9:30 am–6 pm; Friday, 9:30 am–4 pm. Closed Saturday.
Sunday, 10:30 am–5 pm.

This little kosher market on the corner of West Colfax and Utica is almost the last remnant of the old Jewish neighborhood that thrived on the West side years ago. Of course, there's still a small Orthodox Jewish neighborhood here. But there used to be an entire row of kosher shops–a grocery, bakery, meat market, fish market. The Utica Grocery has been in this spot for over 40 years. This is the place to go if you have a yen for gefilte fish, matzoh ball soup, matzoh or Jewish egg bread. They have ten different brands of sardines, fish and kosher meats, which are healthy and free range, without chemicals for the most part. Frozen blintzes, New York-style pizza, cream cheese, apple noodle kugel and kosher cakes are in the freezer. So are half-sour pickles and sliced smoked salmon. On the shelves, you can find canned fruit and fruit compote, juices, marinara sauce, noodles and candles. Stepping into this grocery store is like stepping into another time, when people did all their shopping at the neighborhood groceries instead of at the supermarkets.

Mexican, Caribbean & South American Markets

The Chili Store

4320-C Morrison Road 936-9309
Monday–Saturday, 8 am–5:30 pm. Closed Sunday.

There's a sign near the road, but it's small, so don't drive by too fast or you'll miss out on all kinds of hidden treasures in this friendly and unusual store. It's packed with Mexican and southwestern products, and they're worth investigating. Mixes are many and various, and many of them are made by Valle Grande Products, the company that owns this store. I haven't seen most of these anywhere else. Look for mole or adobo sauce mix, enchilada sauce mix, fajita or sopaipilla mix, mole, tamarind or chorizo hot sausage mix, as well as a wealth of different chiles, like chile cascabel, guajillo, negro, pasilla, de arbol, chipotle and habañero. New Mexico pecan and piñon nuts can be found here, as well as dried shrimp and Anasazi beans. There's masa mixta, the white or yellow masa used to make tamales, as well as blue corn meal, maizena cornstach pudding mix and atole. Sodas include Peñafiel and Jarritos. I also find something else I've never seen elsewhere: cans of jalapeños stuffed with tuna or shrimp filling. There are also bottles of red or green habañero sauce (habañeros are supposed to be the hottest chiles in the world!) and a good selection of hot sauces and salsas. Mexican chocolate, made with sugar and cinnamon, is great to make hot chocolate or to use in desserts. There are large cans of guayabas (guavas) and jalapeños en escabeche (marinated with vinegar and onions) as well as cans of hominy to make posole. Frozen red and green roasted chiles, and frozen tamales, chorizo and masa are great. There's even a wonderful sopa de mariscos soup mix. Don't miss the Chile Store. It's a fun browse.

HANDLING CHILES

Chiles contain oils that can burn your eyes and skin many hours after you've finished handling them. Even washing your hands with soap and water often doesn't get rid of the irritating substance. Wearing rubber gloves is the best way to handle chiles—and wash the gloves and your hands thoroughly afterwards.

ARROZ VERDE CON GUAJOLOTE
Turkey with green rice

1-1/2 cups rice, regular or wild
6 chile poblanos or bell peppers
1/2 small onion, chopped
1 garlic clove, minced
3-1/2 cups turkey broth (could substitute chicken broth)
1 sprig epazote or parsley, chopped
4 large turkey legs or legs and thighs

Simmer turkey legs or thighs in broth to cover 45 minutes. Drain and reserve broth. Take meat from the bones and shred.
Roast, peel and remove seeds from peppers. You can do this either by turning peppers over an open gas burner flame or by putting them under the broiler until charred, turning until each side is roasted. Blend 5 chiles with 1/2 cup of turkey broth. Add onion and garlic and blend again. Sauté rice in turkey fat or a little oil over medium heat, stirring until evenly browned. Pour off any excess fat. Pour onion and garlic mix over rice. When it begins to boil, add remainder of broth and chopped parsley or epazote. Cover casserole and lower heat. Cook over low heat until all broth has evaporated. Rice should be tender. If not, add a little water and cook a little longer. Serve shredded turkey over rice. Cut remaining pepper into strips and use as garnish. Serves 4
Lala's Gourmet Mexican Deli

El Azteca Grocery

1065 Federal Blvd 893-3642
Daily, 8 am – 6 pm. Closed Sunday.

At El Azteca, people line up for their takeout burritos, which have a good variety of fillings. The store offers a small but interesting selection of Argentinian specialties. Yerba maté tea is available, as well as dulce de leche (cream of caramel) in jars, figs and pumpkins in syrup, a sweet potato dessert from Argentina, and an Argentinian quince jam. There are always a few Mexican-style pastries, and small containers of flan in the refrigerator case. Some of the more usual Hispanic products are here as well–dried chiles, large bags of dried beans, masa mixta for making tortillas, chorizo and a rack of spices, many of which are for tea, like manzanilla (camomile), orange flowers and jasmine. I also like the chipotle salsa, which is rather like chipotle ketchup, with that characteristic smoky chipotle flavor. I use it in sauces, salsas and marinades. It's quite hot, but very tasty. But perhaps the best find is Terma, a non-alcoholic apéritif, made with herbs and sucrose. It comes in white or red, and it's absolutely delicious. It has the depth and substance of a liqueur, but with an intriguing herbal edge. The closest thing to it would be vermouth. A real find – just like El Azteca.

Johnny's Grocery & Market

2030 Larimer   297-0155
Monday – Saturday, 9 am – 6 pm. Closed Sunday.

If you're looking for pigs' ears, pigs' tails, pigs' snouts, lamb and hog head meat, brains, tongues, and beef intestines, Helen and Eddie Maestas have them here at Johnny's Market, at the meat counter in the back of the store. They've put in some tables and chairs to serve their customers with the wonderful deli items they make here. They also have specialty items, like the homemade chorizo and carne adovada (spicy marinated pork), as well as homemade menudo and chicharrones (pork rinds), chiles rellenos, and, in the summer, carnitas barbacoa. They make different kinds of burritos every day, and also have steak and chicken ready to take out. In the front of the store are many different kinds of chile, both crushed and ground, and some mixes I haven't seen in other places: spice for menudo, salsa mix, chorizo mix and prepared masa, as well as the corn husks to put it into to make tamales. They have a nice selection of Mexican dried spices, with perhaps more varieties of dried chile than usual: chile de arbol, chile tepin, chile cascabel, chipotle, caribe and pasilla. There is also a fresh vegetable section with tomatillos, fresh jalapenos and other fresh vegetables. All the other necessities for Mexican-style cooking are available too, including beans, posole, lard, and garlic. In season, Johnny's has New Mexico chile ristras and at Christmas they have a great selection of piñatas. I'm sure the market will do well with the addition of an eating area, because all their prepared foods are delicious.

Food in Precolumbian Mexico: When the Spanish invaded Mexico, they were amazed to find that the rich finished off their meals by smoking tobacco and drinking chocolatl, the drink described by Cortez as served in golden goblets and thought by the Aztecs to be the food of the gods.

La Popular Tortillas & Tamales

2033 Lawrence 296-1687
Daily, 9 am–5:30 pm; Sunday, 9 am–3 pm.

La Popular is famous for tamales. It's a family-owned business that's a pleasure to walk into, with a full bakery, including the bolillos or Mexican bread, and pastries like empañadas filled with strawberry, pineapple, apple or vanilla cream filling, and cookies like peanut butter and shortbread cookies with raspberry jam. They also make their own fresh tortillas and on Tuesday and Thursday they have fresh, homemade masa. It's made from dried white corn kernels cooked with lime in copious amounts of water. They have the corn husks to put the tamale dough into, but most people prefer to just buy their homemade tamales. Their selection of Mexican spices is better than the average, with their own brand of green chile powder as well as packets of chile caribe, pasilla, and chile ancho pods. They also sell atole, the corn meal mixture used in soup. At Christmas time, they make a lot of tamales–the demand is incredible–so order early if you don't want to be disappointed.

CEVICHE

4 fillets fresh white fish (orange roughy is ideal), cut into small pieces

MARINADE:
Juice of 10 limes, freshly squeezed
1 red onion, finely sliced
1 head cilantro, leaves only, chopped
1 or 2 jalapeno peppers, finely chopped
Dash salt, pepper, garlic salt

GARNISH:
Small, cooked shrimp
Chopped fresh tomatoes
Chopped green onions

Mix marinade ingredients and pour over fish pieces in a non-reactive bowl (glass or ceramic). Marinate 3 hours. The marinade will "cook" the fish. Serve each portion in a freshly-washed lettuce leaf. Garnish with shrimp, tomatoes and onions. Serve with hot sauce and chips or crackers, if desired. Serves 6–8.
                                          Sabor Latino Restaurant

CHILES

There are over 7,000 varieties of chiles or chilis growing throughout the world. They are totally unrelated to true pepper (piper nigrum) and belong to the genus capsicum, which belongs to the same family as tomatoes, potatoes and eggplant. When the Spanish explorers first tasted chiles in the Caribbean, they thought they were like the black pepper they knew and named them peppers. Some of the most common chiles found in our markets in Colorado are:

Chile Ancho: Ripened, dried chile poblano, can be mild to very spicy

Anaheim Chile: Large, bright green peppers with firm, thick flesh and relatively mild flavor

Chile Arbol: Small, dried, brick orange, very spicy chile

Chile Caribe: Grown in northern New Mexico, a little larger than the pequin. Hot with a sweet, spicy flavor

Chile Cascabel: Small, round chile, sounds like a rattle if you shake it. Pleasant nutty flavor

Chile Chipotle: Dried, smoked jalapeño chile, with characteristic smoky flavor, usually sold canned in adobo sauce. Lala's Mexican Deli smokes their own–and they're sweeter than the canned variety.

Chile Jalapeño: Small, round, dark green and red. Hot to very hot

New Mexico Green Chile: Similar to Anaheim peppers, but hotter. Also found in a dried, red (ripened) form

Chile Pasilla: Brownish-black dried chile, rich tasting and spicy

Chile Pequin: Very tiny, wild chiles. Extremely hot

Chile Poblano: Large, dark green, looks similar to a bell pepper. Usually has a mild, full flavor, but can sometimes be quite hot. When ripened and dried, it becomes known as chile ancho.

Chile Serrano: Small, light green chili, sometimes very thin. Very hot

Thai Chiles: These small dried red chiles are extremely hot.

MILANESA CHICKEN-FRIED STEAK, MEXICAN-STYLE

2 lbs beef steak, thin-cut or pounded thin
1 whole egg
Ground black pepper
Dash salt
Breadcrumbs
Oil for frying

Mix together all ingredients except steak and breadcrumbs. Dip steak in egg wash and roll in any breadcrumbs (Italian seasoned work well). Fry in oil such as soy or olive oil about 2 minutes on each side. Serve with salsa cruda (raw salsa made with tomatoes, onions, cilantro and jalapeños) or any Mexican salsa. Usually served with rice and pinto beans or fried potatoes. Serves 6
Lala's Gourmet Delicatessen

Old San Juan Groceries

664 Peoria   366-5944
Monday–Saturday, 9 am – 8 pm. Sunday, noon – 6 pm.

Exotic food lovers, make tracks for this new Puerto Rican market in the Hoffmann Heights shopping center, across from Helga's German Deli. Pedro Torraca is the brains and the brawn behind this place. He used to work for King Soopers, but realized that there was no market in the whole of Denver where Puerto Rican people can find their native foods, and so he decided to make it his mission to change all that. Vegetables like yuca, yam, chayote, ripe and green plantains and taro can be found here, as well as Cuban squash. Cook them all together, Pedro explains, and you will get a wonderful dish. Yuca is the Spanish word for cassava root or tapioca. In South and Central American countries and the Caribbean, it's a staple, boiled or cut into strips and fried. Many kinds of canned beans, all spiced and ready to eat, are on the shelves. Also, a pleasing number of cold drinks, including a coconut soda, tamarind nectar, and something called Malta India, beloved of all Puerto Rican children, according to Pedro. Corn meal and rice flour can be found here, as well as mole and adobo sauces, sofrito, a base for stews, and cassava and plantain chips. Pedro is already dreaming of a restaurant to augment the grocery store. They sell signs that say "Parking for Puerto Ricaños" and "Parking for Salvadoreños" but everyone's welcome, and they have even begun putting together some recipes so more people can enjoy cooking with their exotic ingredients.

QUICK GUACAMOLE

Mash two ripe avocadoes. Add 1/2-1 cup of your favorite salsa, preferably a salsa cruda that's made with fresh tomatoes, onions, chiles and garlic. Mix well and serve with corn chips.

Middle Eastern & Greek Markets

Arash Supermarket

2159 S. Parker Road   752-9272
Monday–Saturday, 10 am–8 pm; Sunday, 10 am–6 pm.

Pomegranate juice is used in Iranian cooking, so it's not surprising that it can be found in an Iranian (Persian) market. It's also good to drink, and not so foreign to American tastes as the yogurt-flavored doogh you can also find here. Basmati rice, lentils, couscous and bulk fava beans abound here, as well as felafel mix and a fine selection of spices, such as whole anise and cardamom. There's also a large number of different herbs, like coriander, mint, tarragon, leek, parsley and a mixture called ghormeh sabzi, which is used to make a dish of the same name, a thick and delicious stew. Iranian cuisine is very ancient and subtle. Look here for special kinds of coffee, such as coffee with cardamom, or Armenian coffee. There are also several different kinds of tea. Huge cans of cherry and strawberry jam, halvah, tart plum paste and some unfamiliar-looking cookies look interesting. Arash has a small selection of fresh fruits and vegetables. I see little sour grapes, fresh figs, okra and fresh fava beans. In the refrigerator case, there are full milk yogurt, rice pudding with almonds, saffron and rose water, napoleon-like cakes with cream, feta cheese and olives. Huge flat breads look like frozen cardboard, but fortunately don't taste like it. The napoleons are light and creamy.

Aladdin

10315 E. Iliff 337-3121
Monday–Saturday, 9 am–10 pm. Sunday, 10 am–9 pm.

The first thing I notice in this attractive market is the display of charming, small china cups, like espresso cups, with many different designs on them, used for tea or coffee. There's also a large number of different nuts and seeds: salted almonds, salted peanuts, several kinds of melon seeds, including watermelon, honey pistachios and cashews. You'll find a world of olive oil here–Greek, Spanish, Italian and Lebanese, to name but a few, and some in large, three liter cans. Ghee, stuffed vine leaves and tahini are here, as well as huge cans of olives, and some turnip and lemon pickles. Olives abound in many varieties, from the large green olives to the small black wrinkled ones cured in oil. There are even olives with chili, and all seem remarkably reasonably priced. Kashkaval is a cheese found in many countries of the Middle East. It's a smooth eating cheese, similar to the Italian caciocavallo, and can vary from sharp to mellow, depending on where it's from. Find it here and

try it out. Dried apricots and exotic quince jam vie with the pastries in the case for attention from those with a sweet tooth. I can't resist a mix for sahlab dessert, made from a dried orchid root. It's divine.

MIDDLE EASTERN/GREEK FOOD GUIDE

Baklava: A dessert made with layers of phyllo dough, nuts and honey

Basterma: Dried beef coated with spices, sliced thinly

Bulgur: Dried wheat used in tabouli salad or as a substitute for rice

Couscous: Grain made from the heart of durum wheat, finely ground, parboiled and dried

Dolmas, dolmades: Leaves stuffed with meat or rice

Falafel: Seasoned, fried garbanzo bean cakes or balls

Feta: Semi-soft white cheese made from goat's or sheep's milk

Hummus: Garbanzo bean dip, often made with tahini (sesame seed butter) as hummus-bi-tahini

Halva, halvah: A sweet made with flour of various kinds or carrots

Harissa: Hot sauce for North African and Middle Eastern cooking

Kasseri: Firm cheese made from goat or sheep's milk

Kefalotiri: Hard cheese used for grating, equivalent to Parmesan or Romano

Lavash: Round or oval cracker bread

Pita: Arab or Greek pocket bread

Sumac: Seasoning used in North African and Greek cooking

Syrian cheese: Resembles Monterey Jack or Muenster cheese

Tahini: A sesame seed paste or butter

Tarama: Roe of carp used to make dips (can be red or white)

Taramosalata: Dip made from tarama or carp roe

Zatar: Mideastern spice, tasting somewhere between thyme and oregano. Also used for mixture of zatar and sumac

Damavand Market

4101 E. Evans, Unit B   691-2330
Mon–Fri, 7 am–9 pm; Saturday, 8 am–9 pm; Sunday, 10 am–6 pm.

Damavand is another totally fortuitous find, and I'm so glad to discover it. It's right around the corner from the Middle East Market. Mohammad Tehrani, the owner, has many items common to many Middle Eastern stores, and some that are distinctively Iranian. Look for olives, feta and yogurt in the deli case, and huge frozen sheets of lavosh, looking like starched tea towels. There are big bags of basmati rice, as well as dried beans and lentils, and syrups like rose and quince lemon. There are several different kinds of raisins, including golden and what they describe as red, which look like our regular raisins. Different kinds of flour, such as wheat, chick pea and rice, are available, and there are some giant sizes of vinegar, kosher dill pickles, olive and corn oil. Most intriguing are two white sugar cones, wrapped in white net and topped with ribbons of pink and blue. Luckily, I find a customer who can tell me about them. Apparently, at an Iranian wedding, a white satin cloth is held over the heads of the bride and groom and the two sugar cones are rubbed together over it, to ensure that sweetness will bless the union. Isn't that a wonderful piece of folklore? Damavand has a terrific selection of herbs and spices, including the only powdered lemon omani I've found anywhere. Not all the herbs and spices are labeled in English, but the staff is very helpful.

Economy Greek Market

1035 Lincoln   861-3001
Monday–Friday, 7 am–5:30 pm; Saturday, 9 am–5 pm. Closed Sunday.

Economy Greek Market may be the oldest ethnic market in Denver. If it isn't the absolute oldest, it's pretty close. The deli case contains several kinds of cheese, including feta, kasseri (sheep's milk cheese, hard and sharp in flavor), kefalotire and mizithra, a cheese similar to ricotta when soft, and when aged, a fine grating cheese. There are meats like bastirma, a kind of dried spiced beef, and many kinds of olives. There are also sweet, honey-flavored desserts like baklava and kataifi. Behind the counter are bulk spices, some of which are familiar—coriander, whole and ground, dill, whole allspice and sweet basil. There are also some less well-known ones like zatar, a Middle Eastern herb with a taste somewhere between thyme and oregano. I also find molokia, a dried green vegetable used in soups and casseroles that has a consistency similar to okra. Greek taramosalata, grape leaves, capers, in large and small sizes, several kinds of Greek olive oil and many kinds of olives make me start thinking of Greek salads. There are fine, medium or coarsely ground bulghur, fava beans and chick peas, couscous and cornflour and several different kinds of pasta. Most interesting of all are two kits for making desserts: a tiramisu kit, complete with sponge cake and filling, and a profiterole kit. These could be useful for making desserts in a hurry.

GREEK ROASTED CHICKEN

1 roasting chicken, 2–3 lbs, washed inside & out, patted dry
4 Tbsp olive oil
5–6 garlic cloves, halved
2 whole lemons, quartered
2–3 Tbsp fresh oregano, minced or 2–3 tsp dried oregano, crumbled

Brush the chicken with the olive oil, then rub all over with the cut garlic cloves. Place used cloves inside chicken cavity. Squeeze lemon juice over chicken, placing lemon halves inside chicken after. Sprinkle oregano all over outside of chicken. Roast in an open pan in the oven at 325° until juices run clear when pierced.

International Market

2020 S. Parker Road 695-1090
Daily, 10 am – 9 pm.

This is truly an international market, with food from the Middle East, India and Africa, as well as other countries The selection of dried yellow and green peas, fava beans and many kinds of dal–Indian lentils, beans and peas–is spectacular. So is the array of different grains and flour–bulghur, farina, corn flour, rice flour, semolina and roasted gram flour, to name a few. Gram flour is made from Bengal peas, a kind of chick-pea or garbanzo. There is a good selection of Middle Eastern, Indian and other breads–from chapati and pita to lavosh and tortillas. There are many kinds of noodles, ground cassava and cassava flour, Nigerian red pepper, Indian ghee, tahini and felafel mix, and olive oils from Lebanon, Spain and Tunisia. In the refrigerator case is phyllo dough for making baklava, and other great flaky pastries, and kataifi, a kind of shredded wheat-type dough that makes great desserts. They cut and package their own meat, and they have goat and lamb head, as well as more conventional cuts of meat. Honeys are many and various, including alfalfa, wild flower and orange blossom. There are many Indian chutneys and pickles, as well as papads (pappadums) and tandoori paste. The Indian chutneys include such favorites as mango and coriander, and there are syrups and pickles as well. There are many exotic fruit and yogurt drinks. The dessert case is a wonder of small, bite-sized baked goods. A party tray with a selection for $19.95 would feed a large dinner party. I've tried some, and they were flavored with rosewater, delicate and delicious! The International Market has food from almost anywhere under the sun. It's the first place I found that had even heard of ajawan seeds, used in Ethiopian cooking.

APRICOT CHICKEN

4 chicken breasts, boneless & skinless
1 tsp fresh ginger, grated
4 carrots, cut in half, then in 2" lengths
2 potatoes, cut in chunks
1 onion, sliced thinly
1 zucchini, cut in half, then in 2" lengths
24 dried apricots, soaked in water till plump
2 Tbsp honey
1 Tbsp parsley, chopped fine
Pinch powdered ginger
Pinch saffron
4 Tbsp olive oil, divided

Marinate chicken in 2 T olive oil, fresh and powdered ginger, salt, pepper, and parsley. Let sit at least 15 minutes. Barely cover vegetables with water in pan with 1 T olive oil. Cook 30 minutes or till done, with lid off so water can evaporate. Water should be reduced to about 1/2 cup . Add saffron, apricots and honey. Cut chicken in thin strips and sauté in remaining 1 T olive oil if needed. Add to sauce. When everything is heated through, serve over rice or couscous.

Chakhib Marrakchi, Cafe Paprika, Aurora

Middle East Market

2254 S. Colorado Boulevard 756-4580
Monday–Friday, 10 am–8 pm; Saturday, 10 am–9 pm;
Sunday, 11 am–7 pm.

As I walk into the Middle East Market, the first thing I notice is the Turkish delight, figs and dates on the counter. These treats are eaten with tea in many Middle Eastern countries. This is the place to find many Middle Eastern ingredients in bulk: couscous, bulgur wheat, semolina, and split peas, to name a few. There are also many bulk spices: familiar ones like cumin and cloves, and others like seven spices, gram masala (which I buy because it smells so wonderful–like incense) and sumac, that staple of many Middle Eastern stews. There are many different kinds of coffee and tea, from Saudi-style roast coffee beans to ground Turkish coffee, and Twinings tea to Montaz loose black tea. The array of olive oils is extensive: from Italy, Greece and Spain, and there are large cans of stuffed vine leaves and cans of olives. Also, in the deli case, you'll find several different kinds of olives and also feta cheese, including domestic, Bulgarian and French. The sodas are quite exotic, like mango and guava juices and a yogurt soda There is a good selection of Indian chutneys, pickles and curry mixes, as well as the very hot but delicious harissa, a necessary ingredient in many Middle Eastern dishes. Beans, both dried and canned, come in many varieties, such as fava, red beans, lentils, garbanzos and split peas. This is one of the most inexpensive places I've found to buy orange flower water, rose water, and mint water. These waters add a delicate flavor to desserts and other Middle Eastern dishes. Jellies and syrups abound, as well as juices like pomegranate juice. Middle Eastern food is complex and subtly flavored. Here's where you can find all the ingredients for your Middle East feast, except the belly dancer!

COUSCOUS SALAD

2-1/2 cups cooked couscous
2 cups fresh tomatoes, diced
3/4 cup fresh mint, chopped
1/2 cup onion, minced
1/2 cup cucumber, diced
1/2 cup fresh parsley, chopped
1 Tbsp lemon juice
1 Tbsp chopped garlic
1/2 tsp ground cumin
1/2 tsp ground coriander
Salt and fresh cracked black pepper to taste

Mix prepared couscous with all other ingredients. Season to taste with salt & pepper.

David Steinmann, Chef, Barolo Grill

Morocco International Food Market

2690 28th Boulder 444-5587
Monday–Saturday, 8 am–6 pm. Closed Sunday.

Right off Highway 36 that runs through Boulder is this Moroccan food market. It's quite small, but you can still find a large number of Middle Eastern products here. Split peas, green and yellow, are available, as are fava beans, bulghur wheat and olives. Look around for fillo dough, used to make many Middle Eastern desserts, including baklava, and also for kefir and feta cheese There's also pomegranate juice, different kinds of tea and coffee, particularly Gulf-style or Saudi coffee or diwan. Orange blossom honey and Turkish delight are here for a sweet treat, and halawa (halvah), which is also sweet and delicious. Spices like turmeric and anise can be found here, as well as pistachios, and dates and almonds in bulk. Felafel mix and a yogurt dip mix make creating complex dishes a little easier. If you're in Boulder, stop in at the Morocco International Food Market.

Russian Markets

European Mart, Inc.

5225 Leetsdale 321-7144
Tuesday–Saturday, 9 am–7 pm; Sunday, 10 am–6 pm. Closed Monday.

The European Mart has a wonderful selection of foods. The knackwurst, veal brats, Polish sausage, Krakow sausage (a ham sausage), touristenwurst and Hungarian salamis crowd the deli case. Bologna and mortadella are well-represented as well. Next come rows of all kinds of smoked fish–smoked mackerel, whitefish, sturgeon, and sable. There are also several patés, like clam creole paté and paté de foie gras, as well as taramasalata. Dmitry, the owner, insists he has the best price on Beluga caviar anywhere–and I believe him–I'm just afraid to ask what it is! There's a host of cheeses too: Havarti and Swiss cheese, feta from Greece, and cheeses from Georgia, Holland, France and Finland. Prepared foods include blintzes, stuffed cabbage, chopped liver, stuffed peppers and stuffed cabbage. The shelves are lined with jars of marinated peppers, grape leaves, stuffed vine leaves and sauerkraut. There's an orange substance called ajvar, a vegetable spread, delicious on bread or crackers, made from sweet peppers and eggplant. Among the juices, syrups and mineral waters, blackberry, sour cherry, orange, blackcurrant and gooseberry stand out. Big bags of spices fill one shelf: poppy seeds, cloves, whole and ground allspice, caraway seeds and bay leaves. There's another area filled with buckwheat, millet, pearl and fine barley and farina. There are jams and fruits like plum butter, sour cherry jam, greengages in syrup, quince preserves and wild lingonberries in sugar. European-style pastries include poppy seed cake, napoleons and cream cakes, and there are also various chocolates and cookies.

Scandinavian Markets

Big T Market

1700 E. Colfax (at Gilpin) 322-1801
Daily, 6 am–midnight.

Would you ever imagine finding Scandinavian products in the Big T Market? It looks like a regular grocery store on East Colfax, and most of it is just that. But they also stock a number of Scandinavian items. Why? I ask Sheri Barr, who owns the Big T with her husband, Bill. "The previous owner was Swedish," answers Sheri. "He brought in special items from Sweden, particularly at Christmas, and people just expect to find them here. So we carry them too." So, if you're looking for herring, fishballs, caviar, fresh lingonberries (in season), Swedish pancake mix, glogg mix, or Scandinavian syrups, vinegars or mustards, you can find them at the Big T. At Christmas, they have still more: fresh lutefisk, potato sausage, lefse–a kind of flat, Norwegian potato bread–ginger cookies, and sometimes fresh limpa bread and cardamom loaf. Scandinavian foods can also be found at Danish Delicacies.

Specialty Markets, Gourmet & Gift Shops

Alfalfa's

Cherry Creek, 3rd & University 320-0700
Monday–Saturday, 8 am–10 pm; Sunday, 8 am–9 pm.
Capitol Hill, 11th & Ogden 832-7701
Monday–Saturday, 7:30 am–10 pm; Sunday, 7:30 am–9:30 pm.
Littleton, Orchard & University 798-9699
Daily, 8 am–9 pm.
Boulder, Broadway & Arapahoe 442-0082
Monday–Saturday, 8 am–10 pm. Sunday, 8 am–9 pm.

Alfalfa's stores straddle the line between gourmet and natural foods. They're all full-service markets, and you can do all your shopping here if you want. Meat and fish are good quality, though sometimes a little pricier than in regular supermarkets. Vegetables are usually fresh and attractive, and include items not found in regular grocery stores, such as baby vegetables–I recently saw baby sunburst and zucchini squash. The stores also carry fresh herbs, like basil, tarragon and thyme–and also sunflower greens, gotu kola and wheat grass. Gotu kola has medicinal value, and is supposed to give you energy. Unusual vegetables include lotus root, purple potatoes and lychee nuts, as well as several kinds of mushrooms, like shiitake, tree oyster, portabellos and cremini. The selection of salad dressings is enormous, and includes raspberry vinaigrette, fat free and organic kinds. Vinegars run the gamut from London Pub malt vinegar, through mango to rice vinegars, and there's a fine selection of oils too. Honeys, juices, and teas are equally well-stocked and various. The cheese selection is very good, with ten kinds of goat cheese, as well as Brie, feta, fresh buffalo mozzarella and more. The juice bar has everything from Mexican fruit liquados to chai and dairyless choices like soy milk and rice dream. Another area in which Alfalfa's excels, along with Wild Oats, is in the variety of ethnic foods and bulk spices. The ethnic ingredients cost a little more here than if you sought them out in the ethnic markets, but they're all good quality and labeled clearly in English.

Portobello mushrooms 30-40% of cremini mushrooms grow to gigantic size in the same time it takes the regular creminis to grow to regular size. These giants are sold as portobello mushrooms.

Aromas Market

2510 S. Colorado Boulevard   759-0889
Monday–Friday, 10:30 am–6 pm; Saturday, 10 am–5 pm.
Sunday, noon–5 pm. Call, because hours vary with the season.

Here you'll find a better than usual selection of Walker's cookies: not just the ubiquitous shortbreads, but also Walker's chocolate chips and Scottish biscuit selection. The choice of sweet spreads, like jams and maple syrup, is excellent, and there are all kinds, from Tiptree English Christmas preserves to Bonne Maman apricot preserves. The olive oils and wine vinegars are not only many and various, but often in decorative and most attractively shaped bottles. The selection of hot sauces is also good, with some of them having interesting names and descriptions, such as "Tongues of Fire–the unspeakable hot sauce". Besides the store's signature rotisserie chickens, the deli case contains items like Italian meatloaf, shells stuffed with spinach and ricotta, calzones, spinach lasagne, Italian meatballs, roasted red peppers with capers, pesto chicken pasta and twice baked potatoes. For dessert, there's simply cheesecake. There are chocolate truffles, bars of Ghirardelli chocolate and a complete and very pretty espresso bar, with all the different kinds of coffee drinks, and the Italian syrups to go with them.

Denver Buffalo Company

1109 Lincoln   832-0880
Monday–Saturday, 10 am–6 pm. Closed Sunday.

There's a cowboy charm about the Denver Buffalo Company deli, which is sandwiched between the restaurant and the gallery of the same name. Chocolate clusters make a more interesting gift item in their inspired incarnation as buffalo chips. Chile chews are hot candy, and Cherokee Maid pancake mix, pecan syrup and toasted almond syrup promise a flavor of the West. As well as their buffalo bratwurst, salami and hot dogs, they have other deli meats and cheeses. The walls are lined with shelves of salsas and other kinds of Western and Southwestern delicacies like fiery sweet peach salsa, Colorado mud mix (brownies by any other name), black eyed paté and hot pepper salsas and jellies. Chokecherry syrup must be the most flavorful topping ever conceived in the heart of a pioneer cook, and there are other jellies that look almost as luscious – apple, hot pepper and cherry pepper are just a few. Their cowboy coffee is available as beans or they'll grind it for you right on the spot. There are deli sandwiches, many of which feature buffalo, and a good buffalo chili in red (hot) and green (mild). And in case you want to make your own beef or buffalo jerky, there's jerky cure and seasoning in several different blends: hickory, mesquite and Cajun as well as the original. Friends from the East will love this place. It's a taste of the West.

QUITHEO
A Thai noodle soup

1 pkg thin rice noodles
6 cloves garlic, chopped into 1/8" pieces, pan fried golden brown
2 cups shredded cabbage (bok choy, napa or green)
2 cups shredded broccoli stems
6–8 green onions
Soy sauce
Ground white pepper
Sugar
Ground or crushed red pepper
1 lb chicken breast, boneless and skinless
2 anise flowers
1 branch fresh ginger

Put chicken in deep sauté pan. Cover with lightly salted water. Add anise, white part of green onion, and thinly sliced, unpeeled ginger. Bring to a simmer and cook chicken until done. Remove chicken and slice thinly. Cook noodles approx. 30 seconds in broth and remove. Strain and reserve stock. Layer in flat bowls in the following order: chicken, cabbage, broccoli, green part of onion (sliced), soy sauce (to taste) and garlic. Add hot stock to bowls to just cover ingredients. Sprinkly lightly with white pepper and sugar. Sprinkle very lightly with red pepper. Serve while very hot. Serves 4.
   Michael Barnett, Corporate Chef, Armadillo Restaurants

Of the more than two hundred varieties of chile pepper, at least half can be found in Mexico. Most of the heat from chile peppers resides in its seeds and membranes, so removing these can take some of the fire out of the chile.

Garramone's Farm Market

10351 W. 44th, Wheat Ridge 422-0346
Monday–Saturday, 9 am–6 pm; Sunday, 9 am–5 pm.
Closed January, February & the first half of March.

Visit Garramone's for fresh local produce in season, and for many Colorado products like jellies, cider, honey and gelato. Look for chokecherry jelly and syrups, honeys, preserves, jalapeño jelly and Merlino cider. Fresh herbs like dill and baby dill are here, together with Swiss chard and Anaheim chiles, and many other fresh fruits and vegetables. There are lots of spices, salsas, olive oil and balsamic vinegars, often in beautifully shaped bottles, perfect for gifts, and salad dressings and many varieties of La Molisana pasta.

Beans in bulk include turtle, cranberry, adzuke, lima, cannelini and Great Northern. Garramone's has a case of cheeses and other dairy products, and they also have frozen boneless pork chops, sea bass and salmon fillets. Chile ristras add a festive note, and there are southwestern products like hominy and canned menudo. Kathleen and Richard Garramone own and run this attractive market. They sell bedding plants, too, so look for fresh herbs in the spring and early summer to plant in your garden.

Garramone's Fruits and Vegetables

560 S. Holly   320-5561, 320-5597 (24 hour message)
Monday–Saturday, 8 am–7 pm. Closed Sunday.

Jan and Jim Garramone run this gourmet and specialty market on the corner of Leetsdale and Holly. There's a fine selection of fresh fruits and vegetables, including some hard-to-find items like tiny champagne grapes, gooseberries and fresh figs. You'll find a variety of cheeses, the most unusual of which is sheep feta cheese from France. There are lots of relishes, like hot tomato and mild or hot chow chow. Their collection of oils is good: olive, safflower, sesame and canola, to name a few. There are also some gourmet vinegars. One of them is ume plum vinegar. Umeboshe is a small, very tart Japanese plum, so I assume the vinegar is made from them. Preserves and salsas and other gourmet items are always attractively displayed. Everything is high quality.

Greens Market

1312 E. 6th Avenue   778-8117
Monday–Saturday, 8 am–8 pm; Sunday, 9 am–6 pm.

Greens is changing with the times. No sooner did I read that the latest development in grocery markets was for them to serve food in the market like a restaurant, than Greens was doing it–putting in tables and chairs so people can sit and enjoy their foods from the deli case. The food is "healthy gourmet" with lots of vegetarian dishes like couscous and hummus. There many kinds of ethnic foods in the store, including those in the deli and refrigerator cases. Organic produce is a specialty here, and it always seems fresh and inviting. There's also a fine line of salad dressings to go with all these great veggies. Greens has a good selection of both dried and fresh herbs and spices Sometimes fresh dill comes from a woman in the neighborhood. Unusual spices and herbs include camomile, five spice powder and summer savory. They also have Cajun seasoning, and all their herbs and spices are very reasonably priced. The deli case has changing offerings, but might include cold soba noodles, pesto pasta, duck liver pate and hummus. There are also breads and pastries, including one day perhaps a kiwi torte and organic apple pie. The atmosphere at Greens is of a neighborhood grocery store, with helpful staff and attractive products.

Gourmet Foods Warehouse

8223 S. Quebec (at County Line Rd) Englewood 796-7969
 Fax 796-7998
Monday–Saturday, 9 am–8 pm; Sunday, 10 am–6 pm.

Nothing in this place was inexpensive to begin with, so I suppose we can't expect it to be that cheap even at warehouse prices. However, they do have some good deals on things. Gourmet pasta by the pound is here, including a fruit blend: tangerine, lemon lime and raspberry. It's $2.99 a half pound. Different kinds of oils in delightful little bottles include grapeseed, avocado, hazelnut and walnut. There are herb and wine vinegars too, as well as mustards and relishes. Hot sauces abound, some with amazing names. How about Texas Sweat or Endorphin Rush? Soups, like Baxters' Royal Game or Highland Broth look interesting. And when I'm there, they have a sale on Walker's shortbread.

SEAFOOD PIZZA

12"–14" pizza shell
3 Tbsp extra virgin olive oil
2 tsp minced roasted garlic, divided

TOPPING:
2 cups shredded mozzarella
1/2 cup shredded Parmesan cheese
6 medium-jumbo shrimp
4 jumbo sea scallops, split in half
2 oz. roasted red pepper strips
8 artichoke hearts
2 Tbsp chopped fresh basil

Mix extra virgin olive oil with 1 tsp minced, roasted garlic and spread on crust. Sprinkle other ingredients over crust and bake at 450°–500° 6–10 minutes until cheese is bubbly and pizza is golden brown. Serves 2–4
 Jane Myers & Brett Davy, Coos Bay Bistro

PIZZA Pizza was popularized by American soldiers who brought the idea back to the United States from Italy after the Second World War.

Old Santa Fe Pottery

2485 S. Santa Fe Drive   871-9434
Daily, 10 am–6 pm.

If you don't have the time for a visit to Santa Fe, Old Santa Fe Pottery is the next best thing. It's located in an old motel on Santa Fe just south of Evans, and you have to turn into the side street and park behind the buildings. But it's worth the trouble, because it's a really magical place, with a lovely courtyard and all kinds of Santa Fe and Mexican pots and gift items, as well as a great southwestern food corner. Their hot sauces are legion, and include Coyote Cucina, Desert Rose, Tango Papaya and Tango Tamarind. There are many marinades, like the one for flaming fajitas, and a huge selection of chile jellies. Their salsas are amazing too, and the range of their chiles: ancho, caribe, guajillo, pequin, chipotle and habanero. Their Desert Pepper salsas are almost always on sale for $10 for 3, which is a great price. I love the pinto and black bean kinds. They also have Desert Rose salsas, which are very tasty, especially the corn and black bean and the mango. Chile and enchilada sauce mixes? Of course. Ibarra Mexican chocolate? Yes. And many Mexican and southwestern cookbooks. A friendly knowledgeable staff helps, too.

AIGO BOUIDO GARLIC SOUP

6 cloves garlic (or more)
1 sprig sage
1 bay leaf
1 sprig thyme
4-1/2 cups water
3–4 Tbsp olive oil
4 slices bread
1 egg yolk (optional)
Fine noodles (optional)

Peel garlic cloves. Crush or cut in quarters. Place in saucepan with water, salt, pepper, sage, bay leaf and thyme. Simmer 10–15 minutes. Remove herbs. To serve, sprinkle soup with several spoonfuls olive oil. Pour over sliced bread, or stir it, a little at a time, into beaten egg yolk. If desired, fine noodles, like angel hair, can be tossed into the bouillon. Serves 4

Yumiko Baron

The Market

1445 Larimer 534-5140
Monday–Thursday, 6:30 am–11 pm; Friday, 6:30 am–midnight;
Saturday, 8am–12 midnight; Sunday, 8 am–10 pm.

If you haven't sat outside The Market drinking coffee and watching the world go by in Larimer Square, or snuggled inside in the dead of winter, with your hands around a hot drink and your eye out for long-lost friends drifting in from the cold–you haven't lived! The coffee drink list is extensive, and there are all kinds of pastries to go with it–but that's only the beginning. The deli case offers up prosciutto, corned beef, liverwurst, capicola, and cheeses like Gorgonzola, Jarlsberg and Stilton. Hanging around on the shelves that line the walls are the crackers and water biscuits, crisp breads and salsas to complement all these goodies. Add some teas, from Alaskan wild rose to English Typhoo, and you have the beginnings of a tea party. By now it's probably lunch time, so take a look in the prepared foods case for herring in wine, German peasant stew, or one of the many salads: lentil, roasted potato pasta, Caesar or Greek. If you fancy dessert, there's strawberry cheesecake, huge napoleons (a steal at $2 each), crispy Chinese New Year's cookies made of cellophane noodles, chocolate and peanuts, or positively decadent Italian or mango cream cake, huge cream puffs or lemon or chocolate mousse bundt cake. If that's not enough, try the chocolate truffles or chocolate dipped pecan rolls, and pick up some coffee beans to take home as well. The Market is a Denver institution. Long may it last!

Pete's Fruits & Vegetables

5606 E. Cedar 393-6247
Monday–Saturday, 7 am–7 pm; Sunday, 7 am–6 pm.

Walking into Pete's is like stepping back in time, into an old-fashioned greengrocer's, with vegetables still redolent of the earth. All fresh and delicious-looking, his fruits, vegetables and fresh herbs are enticing, making healthy eating a pleasure. There's also a good selection of nuts, like fresh pistachios, raw cashews, piñon nuts and others. Pete has a range of specialty items, including relishes, sauces and pickles. Cheeses include Camembert, Brie, havarti, blue and Montrachet. People rave about his Greek salad dressing, and he also carries hand made pita bread. Don't leave without visiting the bakery next door. Buy some of their great sour cream coffee cake to go with all those healthy vegetables.

Romano's Gourmet Market

1842 S. Parker Road (at Jewell) 755-1005
Monday–Friday, 7 am–6:30 pm. Saturday, 9 am–5 pm.
Closed Sunday.

From cheesecake to pizza bake, and just about everything in between–Randy and Linda Romero have added gourmet ingredients and oven-ready foods to their cheesecake business and presto chango! Romano's is a gourmet market. Pizza is only one of the options they offer. Stuffed shells, baby back ribs, pasta salads, German potato salad and homemade bread pudding are just some of the items in the case when I stop by to case the joint. Dry pastas, coffee, mustards, jams, and hard-to-find delicacies like arborio rice (perfect for making risotto) and paella rice–they're right here! And, of course, there are the cheesecakes: caramel turtle fudge, lemon twist and key lime tarts to make your mouth water. The times are a-changin' at Romano's, so stop by and find out what's new.

Tony's Meats & Specialty Foods

4991 E. Dry Creek, Littleton 770-7024
Monday–Friday, 8:30 am–6:30 pm; Saturday, 8:30 am–6 pm.
Sunday, 10 am–5 pm.

What a fantastic surprise to walk into Tony's. It's an incredible place. "Buon appetito" it says over the door, and Tony's is calculated to give you an appetite just walking around. The place has everything: meats, cooked, like Jamaican jerk pork, or uncooked, or spiced and ready to cook, like fajitas (chicken or beef) and stuffed pork chops. Homemade brats and Italian sausage, wonderful cheeses, including Italian hard ricotta, fresh mozzarella and Asiago. There are also some frozen ready-to-cook items, like rice pilaf and chicken gumbo. Fresh bakery goods, like cupcakes, cannolis, pies, cheesecakes and scones. All kinds of salads, like Maui and Southwestern chicken, and twice baked potatoes, ready to heat! Fresh fruits and vegetables, all of very fine quality. In fact, everything at Tony's is very high quality. It's a good job I don't live close by. Not only would I never cook again, but I'd probably look like the side of a house. Tony's is special. Go and look around. Bet you can't leave empty-handed!

SHRIMP CREOLE

1 lb shrimp, cooked in boiling water, shelled & deveined
1 small onion, chopped fine
1 green pepper, chopped coarsely
1 cup chopped celery
2 cloves garlic, crushed
1/2 tsp sugar
2 Tbsp olive oil
1 14-1/2 oz can Italian plum tomatoes
1 bay leaf
1 Tbsp lemon juice
2 Tbsp hot sauce
1 tsp Worcestershire sauce

Sauté onion, pepper and celery in olive oil. Cook 2–3 minutes over medium heat. Add garlic, tomatoes and juice (chop tomatoes), sugar, bay leaf, and simmer 15 minutes or until slightly reduced. Add hot sauce and remove bay leaf. Serve over rice. Serves 4

Wild Oats Market

2260 East Colfax 320-1664, Daily 8 am –10 pm.
1111 S. Washington 733-6201, Daily, 7 am –10 pm.
12131 East Iliff, Aurora 695-8801, Daily, 7 am –9 pm.
Wild Oats Vegetarian Market, 1825 Pearl, Boulder 440-9599
Daily, 8 am –11 pm.
Orchard & Holly, 796-0996 Daily, 7 am –10 pm.

The Wild Oats on Washington Street is quite fabulous: southwestern in style, very warm and welcoming, and with the feel of a gourmet market more than a health food store. Many items are available in bulk, like lentils, beans and peas, as well as many kinds of flour, including millet, lots of specialty grains, and more kinds of granola than I've ever seen together in one place. Bulk herbs and spices are a specialty here, and they have lots that are very hard to find, medicinal as well as culinary. Their breads are very good (many are from Campagna) and there's a fine selection of salsas and interesting sauces, quite a few different kinds of ethnic foods and also the health food items like miso, tofu, kefir, and many different kinds of yogurt. The other Wild Oats stores have similar products, but the East Colfax store is quite a bit smaller than the others. The Aurora store has recently added tables so you can sit and eat foods in an eating area by the windows. All the stores have gourmet and health foods, very helpful staffs and a pleasant and welcoming atmosphere.

SMOKED SALMON LINGUINE APPETIZER

1/4 pound linguine
3 fresh basil leaves
1 clove garlic
4 oz smoked salmon
1 ounce margarine
1/2 cup whole cream
1 Tablespoon Romano cheese

Cook linguine and drain. Put one ounce margarine and cream, garlic, fresh basil and salt and pepper to taste in a saucepan over medium heat. Let reduce by half, stirring constantly. Add Romano cheese. Mix together and place on plate. Lay the smoked salmon over the top. Garnish with red pepper and fresh basil. Serves 1
                    Kevin Young, Gussie's Restaurant

Gourmet Cookware Markets

Compleat Gourmet & Gifts

7592 S. University Boulevard, Littleton 290-9222
Monday–Friday, 9:30 am – 6 pm; Saturday, 9:30 am – 5:30 pm.
Sunday, noon – 5 pm.

If you're looking for something that'll knock your socks off, head for Compleat Gourmet & Gifts. Not only do they have one of the most complete collections of gourmet pots, pans, products and gadgets in the city, but they also have delicious and interesting gourmet foods, including "religious experience" salsa and "knocks your socks off" spice mixes, for either Italian beef or Italian chicken. Cherchie's products abound, including pretty peppers, champagne mustard and seasonings. Gourmet vinegars, dressings, pasta sauces and spreads like lingonberry and cherry apricot from Scandinavian Delights surprise and delight one and all. They have no less than two old English scone mixes, a bagel mix and even their own brand of gummi grapefruit. And if you're looking for glasses, dishware, or flatware of any kind, it's right across the parking lot at Compleat Selection, their sister store. Pastas in various shapes never seen in Italy, including stars, bicycles and baseball shapes, show up here. A fine selection of cookbooks offers help for almost any kinds of cook, from novice to natural. This is a fine place to go and choose a special gift for someone who loves to cook. Coffee beans and chocolates compleat (!) the picture.

CHICKEN A L'ORIENTALE

  1 chicken breast, with or without skin
  Vegetable oil
  2–3 Tbsp sherry
  1/2 cup chicken broth (homemade preferred)
  1/4 cup Kikkoman soy sauce
  1 Tbsp chopped garlic (or more, if liked)

Brown chicken breast on both sides in sauté pan over medium heat. Add sherry, soy and garlic. Simmer till tender. Serve with steamed rice.

Yumiko Baron

Cook's Mart

3000 E. Third Avenue, Cherry Creek North 388-5933
Mnday–Friday, 10 am–7 pm; Saturday, 10 am–6 pm.
Sunday, noon–5 pm.

Cook's Mart is a wonderful cookware store in Cherry Creek North, with every conceivable kind of saucepan, skillet, bread maker and kitchen appliance. Gourmet foods include a variety of gourmet pastas, including Pasta Mama's tomato basil, spinach and parmesan parsley, and sauces like Italian tomato and creamy jalapeño. Salsas, mustards and margarita mixes jostle balsamic and gourmet vinegars, dirty rice mixes and a fabulous cranberry hazelnut compote with rum. look for salad dressings by the salad bowls and servers and lots of bread mixes by the bread makers. While I am here, someone comes in looking for a part for a coffee maker. The owner generously gives her one from an old model in the store, free of charge.

Creative Cook

1512 Larimer, Writer Square 595-8285
Monday–Saturday, 10 am–6 pm; Sunday, noon–5 pm.
Sometimes stay open later if there are special events downtown.

This is primarily a cookware store, with a nice selection of cookbooks. However they do also carry some gourmet foods. A fascinating jar with four different kinds of pepper is an eye catcher: madagascar green, black tellicherry, white montauk and rose baises each occupy their own little compartment in the gift pack. There are bulk spices, too, in big jars behind the counter: star anise, four pepper blend, powdered mustard and whole allspice, among others. There are lots of nifty gift items, like beer bread mix, cactus marmalade, and a bevy of ceramic salt and pepper shakers. Next door, in the coffee shop, look for espresso drinks, coffees and teas, including jasmine, blackberry and ginger, and more ceramic gift items, like wonderful and unusual teapots, cups and mugs.

Kitchen Nouveau

Southglenn Mall, Littleton   798-9926
Monday–Saturday, 10 am–9 pm; Sunday, 11 am–6 pm.

Kitchen gadgets blossom here in wondrous variety, as well as bread making machines, mixers, juicers and cookbooks. Their gourmet foods center on Colorado products like Kim's gourmet sauces, dried chiles and Colorado salsa. There's also a gift box featuring a mixture of dried mushrooms: morels, porcini and shiitake. Gorgeous jars of marmalade and jam with names like bittersweet orange and wild Maine blueberry conjure up fantasies of breakfast in bed, with a pot of tea, toast and a crackling fire, while outside the north wind doth blow. There are teas, coffee beans and pure maple syrup, as well as bean mixes and flavored oils and vinegars. This is a very attractive, high tech looking store, with a wide range of gift and gourmet items. Gift baskets are a specialty.

ROSEHIP MARMALADE

2 lbs rosehips, with water to cover
1 cup pineapple, diced
1 lemon, thinly sliced
1/2 cup water
5 cups sugar

Slit rosehips in two and discard seeds and any tough flesh. Cover with water and simmer till soft. Press through sieve and measure 4 cups of purée. Add pineapple. Cook lemon in water for 10 minutes, drain and add to purée. Add sugar and bring to a boil Simmer till thick. Pour into hot sterile jars and seal.

Peppercorn

1235 Pearl St (on the Mall) Boulder 449-5847
Monday–Saturday, 10 am – 6 pm, Sunday, 11 am – 5 pm.
Open later at Christmas and during the summer.

Plates shaped like leaves, jugs in the shape of fruits and vegetables, dishes, glassware and whimsical salt and pepper shakers, teapots and cookie jars–this is what you notice first when you walk into the Peppercorn. They have an enormous selection of cookware, gadgets, placemats, napkins–and 10,000 cookbooks as well. Everything for cooking, from blenders to egg timers, can be found here. Look for gourmet foods in gorgeous packaging, and many food gift ideas, including preserves and jams made from exotic fruits like guava, green fig and kiwi. Coffee beans are from Silver Canyon, El Paso Chile Company and Coyote Cucina, among others. Vinegars, oils and mustards are all beautiful and unusual, as are sauces, chutneys and salad dressings. I notice orange and basil salad dressing and gado gado satay sauce. This is a great place to browse–and if you don't find it here, try the Peppercorn Collection across the alley for accessories for bed, bath and home.

Williams–Sonoma

1460 Larimer Street, Larimer Square 534-8300
Monday–Friday, 10 am – 7 pm; Saturday, 10 am – 6 pm.
Sunday, noon – 5 pm.
Also in the Cherry Creek Shopping Center 394-2226

Right on the corner of Larimer & 15th, Williams-Sonoma has an extensive collection of glassware and cookware. Their gourmet foods include many flavored vinegars: for example, mustard seed, five pepper, passion fruit and mango, as well as olive oils, flavored with toasted sesame or dried tomatoes. Oodles of mustards with fancy French names–moutarde verte a l'estragon (green mustard with tarragon), moutarde de cassis de dijon, and spicy peanut sauce. Pastas, fancy pasta flour, bread and scone mixes look tempting. There are jewel-like preserves, including lemon pear butter and blood orange marmalade. Large bars of chocolate for cooking, including their own brand, Lindt and Valrhonna, would make wonderful cakes and candies. There are also teas such as Earl Grey, and even key lime juice as inspiration for making a creamy, dreamy key lime pie.

Chocoholics Only!

Our word "chocolate" is from the Aztec (Nahuatl) word xocalatl, which means "bitter water". In fact, the highly spiced, unsweetened chocolate drink made by the Aztecs from cocoa beans was very bitter, quite unlike the sweet, smooth decadent substance that's considered a luxury and, in some instances, an aphrodisiac, in the western world. Chocolate comes from the beans of the tropical cacao tree. The beans are taken out of their pods to be cleaned, weighed and roasted. They are then removed from their pods, leaving the nibs, which are crushed to extract the cocoa butter from the chocolate liquor. The liquor is refined. Finally, most chocolate is conched or kneaded to create the smooth, delectable texture we love, and other ingredients, including the cocoa butter, are added to make various kinds of chocolate.

CHOCOLATE'S MANY FORMS

Baking, bitter or unsweetened chocolate: Confection made from hardened chocolate liquor and cocoa butter
Bittersweet or semisweet chocolate: Confection made with less chocolate liquor and more cocoa butter
Sweet chocolate: Confection made by adding cocoa butter and sugar to chocolate liquor before the liquor hardens
Milk chocolate: Made by adding milk solids to the sweet chocolate formula
White chocolate: Made from pure cocoa butter, milk, sugar and vanilla. Because it does not contain chocolate liquor, white chocolate is not true chocolate.
Liquid chocolate: Unsweetened and developed for baking, this substance is convenient because it needs no melting. Because it's made from vegetable oil instead of cocoa butter, however, its taste and texture are inferior to baking chocolate.

Chocolate Shops

Blume's Chocolates

6911 S. University, Littleton   795-2506
Monday–Friday, 10 am–9 pm; Saturday, 10 am–6 pm;
Sunday, 11 am–5 pm.

Mary Carol Gleason and her family bought the local outlet of Blum's of San Francisco and it continues to thrive in the Southglenn Mall. Many of the chocolates are hand-dipped. Their most popular item is the meltaway mints, solid chocolate mints that melt in your mouth. Their tortoises (the equivalent of turtles) are also popular, made with caramel and pecans. Sporting and hobby molds like golf bags, golf balls, tool chests, cameras and bowling pins, are also sought-after. Mary Carol herself is usually to be found at the outlet store at 2560 W. Main in Littleton, called Chocolates by Mary Carol, where you can buy Blume's chocolates at a discount. They don't have all the frills, but the chocolates are the same.

Chocolate Foundry

2625 E. Third Avenue   388-7800
Monday–Friday, 10 am–7:30 pm;
Saturday & Sunday, 10:30 am–6 pm.

It smells delicious and looks even more so when I walk into this elegant Cherry Creek chocolaterie. Gorgeous boxes, bags and tins all wait to be filled with yummy chocolates, or are already filled, boxed and bowed ready to brighten some lucky person's day. As well as their own sinfully good chocolates, like cherry cordials, lemon cream truffles, dipped orange slices and dipped oreos and pretzels, the Chocolate Foundry also carries bars of Lindt and Perugina chocolate, instant cocoa mixes flavored with pralines or amaretto and fudge in several different forms: Irish cream, milk chocolate caramel and semi-sweet walnut are just a few of them. The Chocolate Foundry also has a specialty coffee bar, with espressos, cappuccinos and all those good drinks that go so delightfully with chocolate. For Christmas they make fudge mountains and also have topographical maps in chocolate of Aspen, Steamboat, Crested Butte and other Colorado ski areas. Other holiday specialties include chocolate sleighs with bundles, wreaths, cowboy boots and hats.

Cocoloco

1505 Blake 446-8768
Tuesday–Thursday, 11 am–10 pm; Friday & Saturday, 11 am–midnight.
Sunday, 10 am–7 pm. Closed Monday.

Cocoloco is a charming and distinctive place that began as a dessert and chocolate shop and very soon progressed to a restaurant with a full bar and wine list. They have brunch on Sunday, and serve lunch every day but Monday, when they're closed. Their chocolates are outstanding, with truffles like cognac, frangelico and ginger, and 'squirtles', their version of turtles, with chocolate covered caramel. Desserts include several kinds of cheesecake, including lemon and chocolate, as well as key lime pie and napoleons. There are many specialty chocolate drinks, and a nice variety of dessert wines, to be served with all these decadent desserts. My favorite offering is the truffle platter for two: five petite truffles and two glasses of champagne. Is it a test of true love to have an odd number of truffles?

Dietrich's Chocolate & Espresso

1734 East Evans 777-3358 Fax: 623-8203
Sunday–Tuesday, 10 am–6 pm; Wednesday & Thursday, 10 am–9 pm;
Friday & Saturday, 10am–10 pm. Closed Sunday in summer.

Eric Dietrich isn't happy unless he's inventing something new. His latest endeavor is a "truffel torte", which is a chocolate ganache sandwiched between layers of wafers. The tortes come in four flavors –espresso, orange, hazelnut and chocolate. Small tortes are $1.50 and large, party logs are $12. They're simply delicious and go wonderfully with coffee. Eric also serves coffee in his store and has espresso, lattes and other specialty coffee drinks. His chocolates are beautiful to look at as well as delicious and he has many loyal customers who refuse to buy anywhere else. Eric makes his own chocolates and truffles, and makes molded chocolate boxes filled with truffles. His truffle flavors are Grand Marnier, chocolate, hazelnut, espresso and orange cinnamon. At Christmas he has many different kinds of molds, the most popular being the box in the shape of a Christmas tree, filled with chocolates. If you're interested in making your own chocolates and candies, Eric sells block chocolate for $30 for 10 lbs. He makes whipped cream tortes and has chocolate covered liqueurs in Irish cream, hazelnut and kahlua flavors.

THE STORY OF CHOCOLATE

Chocolate is made from the seeds of the cacao tree. This tree is tropical and only grows in hot, rainy climates. Trees take 3–5 years to bear fruit, and are particularly sensitive to wind and hot sun during their first 2–4 years of life. They are often grown in valleys where they can shelter from the wind and sun beneath larger shade trees. Ripened cacao pods look like little footballs and each contain 20–40 cacao beans.

Harvesting cacao or cocoa pods is difficult, because the trees are too fragile to climb. The pods must be cut from the high branches with a cacao hook–a knife attached to a long pole. The pods are opened with a machete and the ivory-colored beans scooped out. The beans change from ivory to purple after being exposed to the air and are placed in boxes to ferment for 2–9 days, depending on the humidity.

After the beans have turned a rich brown, and have begun to smell of chocolate, they are dried and transported to the factories in sacks. The beans differ according to the country and even the plantation where they are grown. At the factory, beans are cleaned, weighed and roasted. The cocoa seeds are shelled, leaving the meat, called "nibs". The nibs are about 50% cocoa butter. The nibs are conched–crushed–for smooth texture. Cocoa butter is extracted and returned at the end of the process. The dark paste left after the butter is extracted is called chocolate liquor.

Divine Temptations

5820 Ogden 296-8212
Tuesday–Friday, lunch 10 am–2 pm, or call anytime to order.

Tammi Davis is the happy, customer-oriented personality behind this multi-faceted enterprise. She bustles around, always busy, but always has a cheerful word to share. Divine Temptations is open for lunch Tuesday through Friday, where she offers five specials, which change daily. She can fax them to you, as she does to many businesses every day. Tammi also makes chocolates–some of the most delicious I've ever tasted–from fall through Mother's Day. They're all hand-made, with no preservatives, and they're absolutely wonderful. Equally delicious is her signature white chocolate cake filled with raspberry purée and dark chocolate mousse. Tammi also makes dinners, from romantic dinners for two to catering for up to 300. For special occasions, like Valentine's Day, she often has dinner packages in different price ranges. In her spare time, Tammi's a hairdresser, so she can cater your party and make you look gorgeous for it too!

Enstrom Candies

201 University (2nd & University) 322-1005
Monday–Saturday, 9 am–6 pm. Closed Sunday.

A local chocolate-maker, Enstrom takes pride in being a leader in the field. Their almond toffee is legendary, and they also have truffles, dipped pretzels, lots of creams, and nuts like dipped almonds, cashews, pecans and macadamias. There are jelly beans and candies and lots of cups, pretty bags and boxes, to pack up your chocolates and candies in. Like many of the chocolate shops these days, they have sugarless chocolates, and theirs taste much better than most. Enstrom's own almond toffee dipped ice cream bars are new, as is their gourmet almond toffee popcorn; both inspired, no doubt, by their almond toffee.

Godiva Chocolatier

3000 E. First Avenue (Cherry Creek Shopping Center) 321-0401
Monday–Friday, 10 am–9 pm; Saturday, 11 am–7 pm.
Sunday, noon–6 pm.

If you want to impress someone with your thoughtfulness and good taste, you could send them Godiva chocolates.

Godiva has a reputation for quality and elegance that's borne out by their tony Cherry Creek location. Everything is beautifully displayed, tempting and sensuous-looking. There are beautifully wrapped and boxed gift packages such as their cordial or deluxe truffle assortment. There are also hand-dipped candied fruits, such as orange rind, looking moist and luscious. Illustrated tins and seasonal packaging make Godiva chocolates an elegant gift.

Hammond Candy Company

2550 W. 29th Avenue   455-2320
Monday–Friday, 8 am–5 pm; Saturday, 10 am–3 pm.
Closed Sunday. (Closed Saturday in summer)

The first thing I notice at Hammond is the giant hand-made whirl suckers on the wall. Smaller versions sit in the window, their colors shimmering in a whirligig pattern. Hammond has been in business over seventy years, making their caramels, creams, chocolate-covered peanuts and macadamia nuts, taffy of various kinds, rock candy on a string and their Rocky Mountain almond toffee. They make mints fresh weekly for special events, like weddings. For holidays, look for their traditional ribbon candy, candy canes and peppermint pillows. Piggy backs, made with caramel and pecans, are also popular. Hammond's own brand of coffee beans comes in flavors of vanilla, Irish cream toasted almond and chocolate, as well as Dudley's and Tante Louise blends.

Lydia's Inc.

7853 W. Jewell, Lakewood   989-5460
Monday–Friday, 9 am–5 pm. Closed Saturday & Sunday.

Lydia's is famous for chocolate roses, and they ship them to stores all over the country. They are really quite beautiful and perfect-looking, in sizes ranging from mini roses and buds through tea roses to long-stemmed beauties, in delicate shades of pink, mauve, rose, apricot, peach, and white. Lydia's also has chocolate tulips and new popcorn lollipops in flavors of green apple, watermelon, butterscotch or cinnamon. There are pretty baskets and cute tins to put the chocolates into and teddy bears to send with the chocolates, so they make a complete gift package. But the roses are what Lydia's is really famous for, and they'll wrap and ship them for you too.

Rocky Mountain Chocolate Factory

7200 W. Alameda, Lakewood 936-8004
Monday–Saturday, 10 am–9 pm; Sunday, 11 am–5 pm.
Also at 1300 Pearl, Boulder 444-8455; 1512 Larimer 623-1887;
8800 Powhaton Mile Rd (Denver International Airport) 342-3472

If you're looking for a walk on the wild side, try the tiger butter, a creamy mixture of peanut butter and white chocolate fudge. Or, if you want something a little tamer, there's the mint-flavored grasshopper bark. At these Colorado franchise stores, much of the chocolate is made at their headquarters in Durango. However, fudge, candy apples and dipped fruits are made in-store. The Villa Italia store has some fun high tech molded chocolate facsimiles: a solid chocolate computer diskette, a chocolate CD and a chocolate Colorado card. Old-fashioned style tins and boxes are perfect for gift-giving for those who prefer a lower tech approach. They have peanut butter cups as big as cup cakes in white and dark chocolates, which will probably please everyone!

Russell Stover Candies

3333 Moline, Aurora 343-9383
Monday–Friday, 8:30 am–5:30 pm; Saturday, 8:30 am–4:30 pm.

For chocolates on a budget, this outlet store is the place to go. There are always bargains here, especially in the summer, which is a slow time for the chocolate industry. While I'm here, there's a sale on a very attractive Whitman's Sampler collectors' tin of chocolates–14 oz for only $3.99. There are also sales on Ambassadors' miniatures collections–they're 50% off, and Easter candies are 75% off. There are even Easter toys like cute rabbits in various sizes and colors for extremely reasonable prices. Truffles and jelly beans can be found here, as well as fudge in several flavors, including vanilla pecan and German chocolate cake. It's a bit tricky to find this store, but bargain hunters will find a way!

See's Candies

875 S. Colorado Boulevard 733-1854
Monday–Saturday, 9 am–7 pm. Sunday, noon–5 pm.

This store is elegant in black and white, with beautiful displays of different chocolate assortments, boxes and novelty chocolate items. Some of their newer truffle flavors are key lime, hazelnut and Mom's apple pie. There are many kinds of creams, caramels and other filled chocolates available by the pound. One of the store's specialties is vehicles with the See's logo transporting chocolates to lucky recipients: a motorcycle and sidecar, a See's truck and train cars are here, as well as a mail box. For those who prefer a more romantic container, there are heart-shaped boxes and tuxedos. See's is also introducing its own Bordeaux coffee, with chocolate and hazelnut flavors as well as the regular coffee flavor.

Stephany's Chocolates

Cherry Creek Mall, 377-7754
Mon–Fri, 10 am–9 pm; Sat, 10 am–7 pm; Sunday, noon–6 pm.
Also in Tabor Center 623-4900; Westminster Mall, 429-7993; Buckingham Mall, 755-4211; 4969 Colorado Blvd, 355-1522 & more

Perhaps best known for the Denver Mint, Stephany's has been making chocolate in Denver for over 25 years. The latest incarnation of the Mint seems to be in packages that say "It's a Boy" or "It's a Girl". A much better idea than cigars, at least! Clusters come in cashew, macadamia, pecan and coconut. The many creams include raspberry, lemon and maple, and there are nougats and caramels as well. Truffles include champagne, the cherry bomb, macadamia, Jamaican rum and white kirsch. They also have many chocolate molds, like cars, planes, tennis raquets, and in a more Coloradan vein, buffaloes, cowboy hats and boots and other such.

Sweet Expressions

1480 W. 104th Avenue, Northglenn 451-1178
Monday–Thursday, 10 am–5:30 pm. Friday, 10 am–7 pm;
Saturday, 10 am–3 pm. Closed Sunday.

Sweet Expressions is a small but lovely store, tucked away in a shopping center in the northern suburbs. Inge, the owner, is very talented, and her chocolate baskets, a chocolate engagement ring and other molded shapes are charming. She has ornaments and popsicles shaped like angels, Santas and Christmas trees for the holiday season, and has been known to put together not just chocolate houses and trees, but even an entire chocolate village. Inge also often has a surfeit of suckers, in shapes like pigs, tulips and flags. Her truffles are delicious. She is originally from Germany, where she learned the art of chocolate-making.

Heavenly Ice Cream

Ice cream was once described as "food fit for the gods". It was probably invented in ancient Rome, improved upon by the French and Italians and popularized by the Americans. Ice cream must have a certain percentage of butterfat to be labeled ice cream. Commercial ice creams usually contain stabilizers to improve texture and body and prevent them from melting too fast. They also contain a certain percentage of air so that they're not so hard.

Sherbert originated in the Middle East in a drink made of sweetened fruit juice and water. It now means a mixture of ice and sweetened fruit juice, and can also contain milk, egg whites and gelatin.

Sorbet never contains milk, and often has a softer consistency than sherbert. An ice is a mixture of ice, sugar and liquid flavoring. It's usually more granular than either sherbert or sorbet.

All for the Better

3501 S. Clarkson, Englewood 781-0230
Monday–Saturday, 11 am–9 pm; Sunday, 2–9 pm.
Winter hours: Closed Sunday.

All for the Better is one of the prettiest little ice cream parlors around; from a distance, it looks like something out of an old-fashioned movie set. They have a good variety of homemade ice cream, including blueberry cheesecake, mocha fudge and the usual vanilla, strawberry and chocolate, as well as sodas, floats, malts and sundaes. Banana splits and sorbet slushes are also on the menu, and ice cream cakes are made to order. Espresso, cappuccino and lattes, with the requisite syrup flavorings, can be found here too. Free refills are offered on Pepsi, Diet Pepsi, Slice, Dr. Pepper, iced tea and lemonade. The place always seems to be hopping, and since it's right across the street from Swedish hospital, that's not too surprising. Homemade soups and sandwiches are available as well as ice cream, and they continue to add more items to the menu. On the wall in the back room is an animal head that I mistakenly identified at first glance as a yak. Silly me! It's a Cape Buffalo, left over from the previous owners, and no-one remembers why it was put there. I suppose it's there because it's always been there.

Bonnie Brae Ice Cream

799 S. University 777-0808
Monday–Friday, 10 am–10 pm; Saturday & Sunday, 10 am–11 pm.

Chocoholics seem to be in the majority at Bonnie Brae. The most popular flavors center on chocolate, like snickers delight, mocha almond chip, oreos and cream or the ultimate in chocolate–triple death chocolate! They have other delightful flavors, too, like cashew divine, blueberry, and banana or mango sorbet. There's a wealth of different toppings all laid out neatly under glass, and you can take your time choosing what you want. There are floats and malts as well as ice cream, and, surprisingly, also milk and butter, just like an old-fashioned creamery. This is truly a neighborhood ice cream parlor–the kind of place to go for dessert on a hot summer evening.

Boulder Ice Cream

1964 13th Street, Boulder 444-6624
Monday–Friday, 11 am–11 pm; Sunday, noon–10 pm.

Flavors here change periodically, but for my visit the options include rum raisin, banana chip, cookies and cream and espresso. I try the last and find it extremely good. There's also an Italian ice sorbet in margarita flavor and many espresso drinks. The place seems a little disorganized, with uncleared tables and flies buzzing about, but the ice cream is first rate.

Ice Cream Makers

1207 E. 9th Avenue (9th & Corona) 831-4010
Sunday–Thursday, 10 am–10 pm, Friday & Saturday, 10 am–11 pm.

This Capitol Hill location has housed an ice cream parlor for over twenty years. Of course, the ice cream here is all homemade. Black walnut, cheesecake, chocolate almond and even oreo are not too unusual. Mississippi mud sounds great. Banana strawberry chip is one I've not come across before, and spumoni's a great idea, but White House is one flavor I can't imagine ever finding anywhere else. It's vanilla ice cream with fruit and nuts. (Insert your own joke here.) One of the most popular innovations at Ice Cream Makers is the introduction of a chocolate chip ice cream cone. You can get gourmet coffee drinks here as well as ice cream. Indulge yourself!

Josh & John's

1444 Market 628-0310
1111 13th St. Boulder 440-9310
Daily, 11 am–midnight; Boulder till 1 am Friday & Saturday.

Josh and John's has some of the best ice cream anywhere. Their stores are bright and friendly and they make their ice cream the old-fashioned way, in modified rock salt and ice freezers. Their ice cream is also sold in many restaurants. Flavors rotate, but some of the possibilities are chocolate chip cookie dough, chocolate white chocolate chip, Colorado cookies and cream, mandarin lemon orange, strawberry and vanilla bean. The service is always pleasant and knowledgeable. It's a pleasure to pig out here.

Liks

2039 E. 13th Avenue 321-1492
Daily, 11 am–11 pm.

Lickety Split, the original name of this ice cream emporium, survives in the name of one of their sundaes, which is a banana split with ice cream and choice of toppings with real whipped cream. Ice cream flavors include piña colada, black walnut, peach melba and amaretto almond. Brandied peach and lemon custard look pretty good as well, but could they ever top my all-time favorite, ginger? Yogurt flavors include key lime, blackberry, peach, and chocolate chip. Not only do they have waffle cones here, they also have waffle bowls, edged with chocolate, if you can stand that much decadence. They have all kinds of soda fountain drinks, malts, coffee and cappuccino. There are tables and chairs outside and inside, so you can sit around and enjoy the many different ice cream delights Liks has to offer.

Also: Moe's Bagels are serving their own homemade ice cream, and Heidi's Bagels and Ice Cream serves ice cream too.

Magill's World of Ice Cream

8016 W. Jewell, Lakewood 986-9968
Monday–Friday, 8 am–10 pm; Saturday & Sunday, 10:30 am–10 pm.

Even if you only crave ice cream once in a blue moon, Magill's is a great place to indulge that craving. They're a fixture in the neighborhood, making a plethora of flavors with that sweet, creamy homemade touch. Blue moon is a tutti frutti flavor, with a really definite blue color. Their other flavors are less startlingly colored. Of course, I had to know what tin roof flavor is, too. It's vanilla ice cream with fudge on top. Not as peculiar as it sounds. Two of their newer flavors are papaya sorbet and watermelon sherbet. Of course, they still have their snowballs, and their O'Clairs, which are Magill's equivalent of ice cream éclairs. Ice cream cakes are available too. Do visit Magill's if you're in Lakewood–it's worth stopping by.

Soda Rock Fountain

2217 E. Mississippi 777-0414
Sunday–Wednesday, noon–9 pm; Thursday–Saturday, noon–10 pm.
Winter hours: Monday–Saturday, 10:30 am–5 pm.

Until it was sold recently, the Soda Rock Fountain was a trip back in time to the fifties–a real old-fashioned soda fountain, with homemade ice cream and a nostalgic feel. The homemade ice cream will still be here, but the place is changing its focus to something a bit more upscale, appealing more to adults and less to kids. The new owner is planning to introduce real fruit sorbets and perhaps add the feel of an old-fashioned candy store, with gourmet chocolates, espresso drinks and desserts, as well as candy. So stay tuned–this place has a great location just off University and close to Wash Park, so it's bound to pop up in a different form, with a new and interesting twist.

One More Cup of Coffee...

There's nothing more delicious than the aroma of freshly-roasted coffee. It's the roasting that brings out the subtle and delightful flavor of the coffee beans. Unroasted coffee doesn't look, smell or taste like the beverage we know. Roasting shrinks the coffee beans in weight, while they double in volume and turn from a pale green to a deep brown color. People often think that dark roasted coffee is higher in caffeine than light roasted beans, but in fact, nothing could be further from the truth. Darker roasts, like French, Italian or espresso, are actually slightly lower in caffeine than lighter roasts. The secret of roasting coffee sounds deceptively simple: it is to roast the beans evenly throughout, so that each part of the bean is equally roasted; to heat the beans for the shortest amount of time and to the lowest heat possible and still achieve a proper roast. This process is entrusted to a roastmaster, whose task is to achieve the degree of roast that will fully enhance the flavor and aroma of each particular coffee. Light roasts generally have higher acidity than darker roasts. Coffee tasters judge coffee by its balance of acidity, body, aroma, finish, flavor, richness and complexity.

Bookend Cafe

1115 Pearl, Boulder 440-6699
Monday–Thursday, 6:45 am–11 pm; Friday & Saturday, 6:45–midnight; Sunday, 6:45 am–9 pm. Closes 1 hour earlier in winter.

Real tea, which means loose tea instead of teabags, is a real treat at this pleasant brick and wood cafe next door to the Boulder Bookstore. The Greek pizza is delicious, and they have all manner of sandwiches, like chipotle chicken, salads galore, and also bao–Chinese style buns. The black bean one is good. Next time, perhaps the pork? Desserts look inviting, too, with raspberry chocolate nut cake, raspberry Linzer bars, muffins, lemon bars, croissants and lots more. Oh–and they have great coffee, too!

Boyer's Coffee Company

747 S. Colorado Boulevard (Belcaro Shopping Center) 289-3345
Monday–Friday, 6 am–7 pm; Saturday, 7 am–7 pm. Closed Sunday.
6820 S. University Boulevard 289-3345
Monday–Friday, 6 am–6 pm. Saturday, 7 am–6 pm. Closed Sunday.
7295 N. Washington 289-3345
Mon–Fri, 6:30 am–5:30 pm; Saturday, 8 am–2 pm. Closed Sunday.

Boyer's probably has the best prices in town for coffee. They always have sales on different items, and a discounted flavor of the month. All stores have a large variety of coffees, including a large number of flavored coffees. Bulk teas and spices are also available. Some of their spices are fairly unusual, such as hibiscus flowers, juniper berries and lavender flowers. All the stores also have books about coffee, tea and spices. A full line of accessories includes coffee grinders, coffee pots, mugs, cappuccino machines and tea infusers and strainers, to name a few. All the stores put together gourmet gift baskets and boxes, either combinations that they dream up themselves or put together to their customers' specifications. Mail order catalogs are available at all Boyer's stores.

Caffé Arabica

2200 Kearney Street 333-2401
Monday–Thursday, 7 am–9 pm; Friday, 7 am–10 pm;
Saturday, 8 am–10 pm. Sunday, 8 am–6 pm.

Caffé Arabica has become quite a neighborhood hangout in Park Hill. You can sit in the comfortable room, with its teal and black tables and chairs, and watch through the huge plate glass windows for your friends to arrive on bicycles, pushing strollers or dragging the family hound. The coffee they serve as lattes or cappuccinos or sell as coffee beans is Silver Canyon. The menu has expanded over the last year to include more sandwiches, pot pies, scones, muffins, bagels, danishes and biscotti. The cafe serves steamers, hot milk flavored with Italian syrups, and Italian sodas, and, in summer, iced coffee drinks and Liks ice cream. And, perhaps best of all, there's a games section for kids and adults. Puzzles and games are just sitting there, waiting for anyone in need of a little light amusement to come by and get them down off the shelf. This is an attractive little neighborhood place, with a warm and friendly atmosphere. It would be hard not to feel at home here.

Colorado Espresso Company

2075 S. University 744-2531
Monday–Thursday, 6:30 am–10 pm; Friday, 6:30 am–11 pm;
Saturday, 7:30 am–11 pm; Sunday, 8 am–6 pm.

Colorado Espresso is a really comfortable place to hang out. It's in the DU area, right by the corner of Evans and University, set back from the street a bit in a row of small shops. The feeling of the coffee shop is open and welcoming. Debi Joens, who owns the place, is extremely knowledgeable about coffee in all its aspects. And so she should be–the reason she opened Colorado Espresso was that she was sick of searching all over Denver for a skinny latte! Shortbread, florentines, lemon bars, scones and cookies, as well as poppy seed and banana bundt cakes, are ideal for munching on with your latte or cappuccino. Sandwiches are becoming more varied as Debi finds out what her customers are looking for. In the summer, try granita in the traditional coffee flavor, or in the flavor of the day. Gelato bravo, a local brand of gelato, is also an option. In winter, steamers or other hot coffee drinks will stave off the winter winds. There are art shows here that change monthly, and entertainment every Friday night from 8–10 pm. On the counter is a jar labeled "doggie biscotti". They're really just dog biscuits, but it's a cute idea. Debi serves Seattle's Best Coffee, and to many, Denver's best as well.

Common Grounds

3484 W. 32nd Avenue 458-5248
Monday–Thursday, 6:30 am–11 pm; Friday, 6:30 am–12 midnight;
Saturday, 7:30 am–midnight; Sunday, 7:30 am–11 pm.

Coffee should be hotter than hell, stronger than death, and sweet as love. So says the motto on the counter in this reminder of college hangouts from the past, a big barn of a place with wood floors, and a friendly atmosphere with games and newspapers that encourage you to stay a while and talk, socialize and enjoy. Actually, there are several interconnected rooms, with bookshelves, tables and chairs scattered around them. This is a neighborhood coffee house, serving snacks and light lunches as well as lattes, espressos, cappuccinos and other coffee drinks. It's a pleasant place to sit and drink coffee, with huge windows, a few tables outside in the summer and an area of toys and games for children. They have great cookies, scones and muffins.

Java Creek

287 Columbine (3rd & Columbine) 377-8902
Monday–Saturday, 7 am–10 pm; Sunday, 8 am–5 pm.

The coffee here is as good as any you'll get in Denver, and the sandwiches and scones (especially those homemade scones!) are probably better. But what really keeps people coming back to Java Creek is the atmosphere. How to describe it? It's like spending time at a good friend's house, knowing you can drop in whenever you want to and you'll always be welcome.

You can read the newspapers and magazines and indulge in some of the great homemade knishes, shepherd's pie, quiche or sandwiches. All espresso drinks, plus tea and chai are available. Pull up a chair and stay awhile.

Java Hut

6603-C Leetsdale Drive (Monaco & Leetsdale) 333-0655
Monday–Friday, 6 am–5:30 pm; Saturday, 7 am–4 pm;
Sunday, 8 am–2 pm.

It's not fancy, but it's nice, with the usual gourmet coffee drinks, and a new Italiano menu. I walk in, and it smells of garlic rather than coffee. They must be cooking up something like the Napoli: fontina cheese, baked eggplant, sun-dried tomatoes, garlic and artichoke hearts, served on fresh focaccia bread. They have scones and muffins, bagels and croissants, and their prices re really reasonable. This is another place where you can hang out and read their newspapers and magazines with out fear of reprisals. In fact, the staff is pleasant, helpful and welcoming. They display a larger than usual selection of coffee beans. If you don't like coffee, try the live chai or one of the other alternative drinks.

Jitters Internet Cafe

1523 18th St. 298-8490
Monday–Friday, 6:45 am–midnight. Saturday, 9 am–midnight or 1 am; Sunday, 9 am–9 pm.

There are more teas here than coffees (over 200 of them, in fact), from Goddess and Japanese Blessing to Sport Tea. Lattes and espressos are here, as well as light snack foods. But the real draw is the on-line time that you can buy by the 1/2 hour and up. There's a pleasant, almost rundown feel to this place, with an old couch up front where people stretch out and snooze, tables along the walls and four computer terminals in the back. Next to the terminals is a teddy bear. Just like home?

Latta's Espresso Company

300 East Sixth Avenue, #5 (6th & Grant)   733-1114
Monday–Friday, 6:30 am–7 pm; Saturday, 7 am–7 pm; Sunday, 8 am–3 pm.

On the corner of 6th & Grant, Latta's is the place where media people often stop to get their morning coffee. It's a very high tech, industrial-looking environment, without being in the least unwelcoming. The furniture is minimalist: steel, pink and turquoise, and part of the concrete floor is covered with a multi-colored area rug. They serve Torrefazione coffee, and have bagels from Finster Brothers. Try their macchiato (espresso with foam), steamed cider or cremosa, which is Italian soda with cream. Latta's is one of the few places I've seen that serves cambric tea, something I thought was only drunk by Victorian heroines in books. It's made with tea and steamed milk. How very genteel!

The Market

1445 Larimer 534-5140
Monday–Thursday, 6:30 am–11 pm; Friday, 6:30 am–midnight;
Saturday, 7:30 am–midnight; Sunday, 8 am–10 pm.

When the West was first being settled, people came into town and met at the general store. The Market has retained the atmosphere of the old general store, but the merchandise is strictly specialty and deli food. You can sit outside or in, and eat, people-watch or examine the selection of cookies, candies, vinegars, teas and other items that line the walls. They have the usual specialty coffee drinks and some good muffins and pastries. See also listing under Markets.

The Neighborhood Buzz

4339 West 44th Avenue (44th & Tennyson) 458-8051
Monday–Thursday, 6:30 am–10 pm; Friday, 6:30 am–10 pm.
Saturday & Sunday, 8 am–10pm.

Zim just took over this neighborhood coffee shop, so hours are tentative until he figures out what will work. They serve fresh & locally roasted coffee, and offer a number of espresso drinks, including the house specialty, grande mocha: espresso & Hershey's syrup with steamed milk topped with whipped cream. Bagels from Heidi's Bagels and cakes and pastries, mostly from North Denver bakeries, are available here. Assorted sandwiches are served, and if you don't like coffee, hot chocolate, sparkling waters, teas, both hot and iced, and other beverages, like Italian sodas and blended drinks, will be more than adequate substitutes. The cafe is relaxed and cheerful and so is the staff. Stop in if you're in the neighborhood.

Old World Coffee & Tea Company

1512 Larimer Street, Writer Square 595-8285
Monday–Friday, 8 am–6 pm; Saturday, 10 am–6 pm;
Sunday, noon–5 pm. Open later if there are events downtown.

An adjunct to the Creative Cook gourmet store, this coffee bar (it has a couple of bar stools, but it's mostly takeout) has a large variety of coffee beans, from cappuccino Italiano and hazelnut to snickerdoodle (can coffee really taste like that?) to roasts named after some of Denver's late and/or great restaurants (Dudley's, Brown Palace and Cliff Young's). Teas include jasmine, blackberry and ginger, and there's also a plethora of pretty boxes of various herbal teas. Teapots suitable for gifts or collecting, coffee and tea mugs and cups, and a full range of coffee and tea specialty drinks round out this small but jam-packed with goodies store.

Paris on the Platte

1553 Platte Street   455-2451
Monday–Thursday, 11 am–1 am; Friday, 11 am–4 am;
Saturday, noon–4 am; Sunday, 7 am–1 am.

The signature drink here is called Cafe Fantasia, and it's made of hot chocolate, steamed milk and espresso, poured over a fresh orange slice, topped with whipped cream and grated orange peel. It's delish. Cafe Mexicana is also popular, made with hot chocolate, espresso, steamed milk and cinnamon. This is a bookstore as well as a coffee shop, and people tend to sit around here, talking, reading and studying. The only no-smoking section in the store is in the bookstore. You can get soups, sandwiches, scones, cookies and muffins here. Perhaps it's the smoke, but it reminds me of the coffee houses of the sixties. Does anyone know any protest songs?

Peaberry Coffee Ltd.

5070 E. Arapahoe Road (at Holly, near King Soopers)   741-1303
Mon–Fri, 6:30 am–8 pm; Saturday, 7:30 am–8 pm; Sunday, 8 am–6pm.
Also at: 2721 Arapahoe Avenue, Boulder   449-4111
3031 E. 2nd Avenue (2nd & St. Paul)   322-4111
1685 S. Colorado Boulevard   756-4111;
1201 16th Street (Tabor Center)   595-4111;
1685 S. Colorado Blvd.   756-4111

All the Peaberry Coffee shops are very attractive and upscale. Their coffee is fresh roasted daily, and I find it superior in taste. Beans range from Ethiopian Yergacheffe to Mocha Yemen to Kona Peaberry, which is over $20 per pound. They have many flavored coffees, like hazelnut and German chocolate cake. Try one of their croissants, bagels, low fat cookies or low fat cinnamon sticks with your coffee. There are many coffee makers, espresso makers and other coffee paraphernalia, including a Nissan stainless steel thermos that keeps coffee hot for 6 hours.

Penny Lane

1795 Pearl Street, Boulder 443-9516
Daily, 6 am–midnight.

The decor here can best be described as voodoo cafe. There's voodoo paraphernalia around, including Mardi Gras throws and bones hanging from the ceiling. Incense burns on the counter. This is a hip hangout for those with pierced body parts, but you won't feel unwelcome if you're less trendy.

You'll find coffee drinks, teas of many kinds, like Ceylon, Darjeeling, and Earl Gray, and Izzy's fizzies: fruit, ice, Torani syrup and carbonated water. Snack on pastries and cakes and bagels and sit on the outdoor patio if the weather cooperates.

OLD-FASHIONED COFFEE SODA

3 cups chilled double-strength coffee
1 Tbsp superfine sugar
1 cup half-and-half
1 pint coffee ice cream
3/4 cup chilled club soda
Sweetened whipped cream for garnish

Combine coffee and sugar in large jug. Blend in half-and-half and fill 4 soda glasses half full with the mixture. Add dollop of ice cream to each glass and fill with soda. Top with whipped cream if desired. Serves 4.

Boyer's Coffee

St. Mark's Coffee House

1416 Market Street 446-2925
Monday–Thursday, 7 am–midnight; Friday & Saturday, 7 am–1 am.
Sunday, 8 am–midnight.

Young, hip and fun, St. Mark's is the place to meet friends, sit outside and chat when the weather's fine, and study or read if you want. It's a rather bare concrete space, broken up into several rooms and decorated with whimsical chairs, tables and a gallery of changing art on the walls. They make all their baked goods here, including banana cake, orange pound cake, peach tarts, German cream cheese brownies and more. Sandwiches are available, and there are all the usual suspects in the coffee and tea department. In spite of the trendy lower downtown location, I get the feeling you could hang out here all day and no-one would bother you. It's great.

Starbucks

2701 East 3rd Avenue (3rd & Clayton) 331-9910
Monday–Saturday, 6:30 am–9 pm; Sunday, 7 am–7 pm.
Also at: 2nd & Fillmore 388-7565; Arapahoe & I-25 689-0728
6200 S. Syracuse Way, Greenwood Village 721-7611
Quebec & County Line Road 779-5221 & more.

Espressos, cappuccinos, lattes and a bunch of other drinks including steamed milk or cider beckon from these Seattle transplants that have sprung up all over Denver. There's also a variety of teas and herbals, like Earl Grey and jasmine tea, offered to complement the croissants, scones, coffee cake and other edibles. You can save 10% if you bring your own mug (it's also good for the ecology) and coffee beans are for sale. I try some of the gazebo blend, a mixture of Arabian and African coffees. It's "the best year yet" for this particular blend, according to Bruce. Well, fine wine and coffee connoisseur I'm not, but it's a very amusing little coffee!

Terra of the Earth

8525 W. Colfax 274-2697
Monday–Wednesday, 6:30 am–10 or 11 pm; Thursday, Friday & Saturday, 6:30 am–midnight-2 am; Sunday, 9 am–8 pm.

Delightfully eclectic is my description of Terra of the Earth. Easy chairs, pictures on the walls, even a faux fireplace– in the back room of this coffee house, it feels like being in someone's living room. In the front, there are tables and chairs, more like the usual coffee shop, but the welcoming feeling is the same. To get into the place, however, you pass a couple of counters filled with jewelry–just in case you need a silver ring or a New Age-style pendant. Panino sandwiches are sold here, as well as pastries and a selection of coffee drinks. Live entertainment nightly ranges from rock, flute, folk and instrumental jazz to new age. They're starting poetry nights on Tuesday evenings.

Trident Booksellers & Cafe

940 Pearl, Boulder 443-3133
Monday–Friday, 6:30 am–11 pm; Saturday & Sunday, 7 am–11 pm.

Coffee drinks, including hot chocolate florentine, (coffee and chocolate), lattes, and cappuccino orzata, coffee with a shot of almond syrup, can be consumed in a very relaxed atmosphere. Desserts like walnut chocolate chip bar (highly recommended!) shortbread, and other good desserts, are also available. The bookstore's right next door for browsing.

A SHORT HISTORY OF COFFEE

It's widely believed that coffee was discovered by Ethiopian tribesmen, who ate the coffee berries they found while tending their herds. It wasn't until the use and cultivation of coffee spread to Arabia that it was steeped in water to make a delicious drink. By the thirteenth century, coffee was being shipped from Arabian ports like Mocha, but there was a ban on the export of coffee seeds and plants. By the end of the fifteenth century, Arabian coffee houses were flourishing, and coffee had become part of daily life. It's rumored that a Moslem pilgrim managed to smuggle a coffee plant or seeds into India in the 17th century, and the cultivation of coffee quickly spread. Coffee was introduced into Europe by Venetian merchants and English coffeehouses became the center for intellectual and political discussions. A French naval officer is said to have stolen a coffee plant from Louis XIV's hothouse in Paris and introduced it to the Caribbean, and from there it spread throughout the islands and South America. In the U.S., tea was the beverage of choice until the boycott of English tea that culminated in the Boston Tea Party. After that, coffee became popular and has remained the most popular American beverage ever since!

And for all you tea lovers...

Celestial Seasonings Tea Shop, 4600 Sleepytime Drive, Boulder, offers a great free tour of the tea manufacturing plant and herb garden, ending up in the shop and tasting room where you can taste any tea you please, and buy teas and other gift items. Call 581-1202 for directions to the plant from Denver and Boulder. The peppermint room will leave you breathless!

STORE INDEX

A Piece of Cake, 5
Air–Afrik, 71
Aladdin, 108
Alfalfa's, 117
All For The Better, 140
Alpine Sausage, 45
André's Confiserie Suisse, 28
Arash Supermarket, 107
Aromas Market, 118
Asian Deli, 72
Asian Market, 72
Bagel Brothers, 17
Bagel Deli, 56
Bagel Nook Nook South, 18
Bagel Store, 19
Baker's Street, 6
Belfiore's Italian Sausage, 49
Bender's Brat Haus, 46
Black Forest Specialties, 92
Bluepoint Bakery, 6
Blume's Chocolates, 133
Bobby Dazzler, 7
Bolo Bagel Bakery, 18
Bombay Bazaar, 93
Bonjour Bakery, 7
Bonnie Brae Ice Cream, 141
Bookend Cafe, 144
Boulder Ice Cream, 141
Boyer Coffee Company, 145
Breadworks, 33
Caffé Arabica, 145
Campagna, 33
Canos Collection, 87
Carbone Italian Sausage, 50
Caribbean Bakery, 23
Celestial Bakery, 16
Chateau de Patisserie, 21
Cheese Company, 70
Cherry Crest Market, 65
Child's Pastry Garden, 8
Child's Pastry Shop, 8
Chili Store, 101
Chocolate Foundry, 133
Cocoloco, 134

Colorado Espresso, 146
Common Grounds, 146
Compleat Gourmet & Gifts, 128
Continental Deli, 46
Cook's Mart, 129
Cosolo's Market, 97
Creative Cook, 129
Cucina Leone, 51
Daily Bread, 8
Dale's Exotic Game Meats, 66
Damavand, 110
Daniel's of Paris, 24
Danish Delicacies, 22
Das Meyer Pastry Chalet, 29
Dave-Pan Bagel Bakery, 19
Deli Italia, 51
Denver Buffalo Company, 118
Denver Oriental Supermkt, 74
Dietrich's Chocolate, 134
Dimmer's Home Bakery, 29
Divine Temptations, 136
East Coast Italian Deli, 42
East Side Kosher Deli, 57
Economy Greek Market, 111
El Alamo Bakery, 30
El Azteca Grocery, 109
English Teacup, 88
Enstrom Candies, 136
European Bakery, 34
European Delights, 45
European Gourmet, 61
European Mart, 115
Evergreen Pastry Shop, 9
Finster Brothers, 19
Fratelli's, 9
Fred's Fine Meats, 66
Gargaro's Bakery, 34
Garramone's Farm Market, 120
Garramone's Fruits & Veg. 121
Gaspare's Bakery, 29
Godiva Chocolatier, 136-7
Gourmet Foods Warehouse 122
Granny Scott's Pie Shop, 10
Great Harvest Bread Co., 10

Greens Market, 121
Hammond Candy Co., 137
Heidi's Bagels & Ice Cream, 20
Helga's German Deli, 47
Herb's Meats & Specialty, 66-67
House of Windsor, 89
Ice Cream Makers, 141
Indochina Enterprises, 74
International Market, 112
Jacobs Bagelry, 20
Java Creek, 147
Java Hut, 147
Jitters Internet Cafe, 148
Johnny's Grocery & Mkt., 103
Josh & John's Ice Cream, 142
Just From Scratch, 11
Karen's Country Kitchen, 12
Karl's F.F. Delicatessen, 48
Kitchen Nouveau, 130
Korean Rice Cake, 17
Krungthai, 76
La Favorita, 36
Lala's Gourmet Mexican, 60
Laotian Oriental Food Store, 76
La Patisserie Française, 24
La Popular, 104
Latta's Espresso Company, 148
Le Bakery Sensual, 41
Le Délice, 25
Le Français, 26
Lek's Asian Market, 77
Lemon Cheese Company, 90
Lick Skillet Bakery, 13
Liks Ice Cream, 142
Little Saigon Supermarket, 78
Lonardo's Italian Deli, 52
Louisiana/Texas Catfish, 67
Lydia's Inc., 137
Magill's World of
   Ice Cream, 142
Mama Pirogi's, 23
Manna Bakery, 13
Market, The, 124, 149
Mekong, 79
Mexidans, 36
Middle East Market, 113

Midopa Market, 79
Moe's Broadway Bagels, 21
Morocco Food Market, 114
Mortensen's Gourmet, 43
Neighborhood Buzz, 149
New York Bagel Boys, 21
New York Deli News, 57
Nina's Deli, 62
Nipa Hut, 91
Nonna's, 35
Old Fashioned Bavarian, 30
Old Fashioned Italian Deli, 53
Old San Juan Groceries, 106
Old Santa Fe Pottery, 123
Old World Tea & Coffee, 149
Oliver's Meat Market, 68
Omi & Pa's, 49
Omonia Bakery, 28
Oriental Food Market, 81
Oriental Grocery Store, 82
Oriental Market, 82
Pacific Mercantile, 83
Pacific Ocean Marketplace, 84
Panaderia Aguas Calientes, 36
Panaderia El Alamo, 37
Panaderia Guadalajara, 38
Panaderia La Chiquita, 38
Panaderia y Pasteleria
   Santa Fe, 39
Panaderia Rodriguez, 40
Pantry Basket, 13
Paris Bakery, 27
Paris on the Platte, 150
Pasta Pasta Pasta, 64
Pasteleria del Norte, 40
Peaberry Coffee Ltd, 150
Penny Lane, 151
Peppercorn, 131
Pete's Bakery, 14
Pete's Fruits & Vegetables, 132
Plaza Deli, 58
Rheinlander Bakery, 30
Roberto's Sausage, 54
Rockies Deli & Bakery, 43
Rocky Mtn. Choc. Factory, 138
Romano's Gourmet Market, 125

Rosales Mexican Bakery, 41
Rosen's Deli, 59
Russell Stover Candies, 138
St. Mark's Coffeehouse, 151
Salvaggio's Italian Deli, 54
Sam's Meat Market, 68
Scratch Baked, 14
See's Candies, 138-9
Seoul Oriental Market, 84
Sir Loin Meat Shoppe, 68-69
Soda Rock Fountain, 143
Spinelli's Market, 98
Spruce Confections, 15
Starbucks Coffee Co., 152
Star Market, 44
Staropolska Deli, 62
Stephany's Chocolates, 139
Sugar-Less Sensations, 14-15
Sweet Expressions Inc., 139
Sweet Soiree, 24
Tajmahal Imports, 95
Tan PhatOriental Market, 85

Tedi's Polish Deli, 63
Tejal International Foods, 95
Terra of the Earth, 152
The Cheese Company, 66
The Market, 124, 149
Tony's Italian Sausage, 55
Tony's Meats & Specialty
   Foods, 126
Trident Booksellers, 153
Uncle Milt's Fine Meats, 69
Utica Grocery, 100
Valente's Deli Bakery, 55
Vinh Xuong Bakery, 17
Vinnola's Italian Market, 98
Vollmers Bakery, 15
Wally's Quality Meats, 69
Wild Oats Market, 127
Williams-Sonoma, 131
Xuan Trang, 87
Zaidy's Deli, 59

INDEX BY STORE TYPE

BAKERIES

A Piece of Cake, 5
André's Confiserie Suisse, 28
Bagel Brothers, 17
Bagel Nook/Bagel Nook S, 18
Bagel Store, 19
Baker's Street, 6
Bluepoint Bakery, 6
Bobby Dazzler, 7
Bolo Bagel Bakery, 18
Bonjour Bakery, 7
Campagna, 33
Caribbean Bakery, 23
Celestial Bakery, 16
Chateau de Patisserie, 21
Child's Pastry Garden & Child's
   Pastry Shop, 8
Daniel's of Paris, 24
Danish Delicacies, 22

Das MeyerPastry Chalet, 29
Dave-Pan Bagel Bakery, 19
Dimmer's Home Bakery, 29
European Bakery, 34
Evergreen Pastry Shop, 9
Finster Brothers, 19
Fratelli's, 9
Granny Scott's Pie Shop, 10
Great Harvest Bread Co., 10
Heidi's Bagels & Ice Cream, 20
Jacobs Bagelry, 20
Just From Scratch, 11
Korean Rice Cake, 17
La Favorita, 36
La Patisserie Française, 24
Le Bakery Sensual, 41
Le Délice, 25
Le Français, 26
Lick Skillet Bakery, 13
Mama Pirogi's, 23

Manna Bakery, 13
Mexidans, 36
Moe's Broadway Bagels, 21
New York Bagel Boys, 21
Nonna's, 35
Old Fashioned Bavarian
  Bakery, 30
Omonia Bakery, 28
Panaderia Aguas Calientes, 36
Panaderia El Alamo, 37
Panaderia Guadalajara, 38
Panaderia La Chiquita, 38
Panaderia y Pasteleria
  Santa Fe, 39
Panaderia Rodriguez, 40
Pantry Basket, 13
Paris Bakery, 27
Pasteleria del Norte, 40
Pete's Bakery, 14
Rheinlander Bakery, 30
Rosales Mexican Bakery, 41
Scratch Baked, 14
Spruce Confections, 15
Sugar-Less Sensations, 14-15
Sweet Soirée, 24
Vinh Xuong Bakery, 17
Vollmers Bakery, 15

DELICATESSENS

Alpine Sausage Co., 45
Bagel Deli, 56
Belfiore's Italian Sausage, 49
Bender's Brat Haus, 46
Carbone Italian Sausage, 50
Continental Deli, 46
Cucina Leone, 51
Deli Italia, 51
East Coast Italian Deli, 42
East Side Kosher Deli, 57
European Delights, 45
European Gourmet, 61
Helga's German Deli, 47
Herb's Meats & Specialty
  Foods, 66
Karl's F.F. Delicatessen, 48

Lala's Gourmet Mexican, 60
Lonorado's Italian Sausage, 52
Mortensen's Gourmet, 43
New York Deli News, 57
Nina's Deli, 62
Old Fashioned Italian Deli, 53
Omi & Pa's, 49
Plaza Deli, 58
Roberto's Sausage, 54
Rockies Deli & Bakery, 43
Rosen's Deli, 59
Salvaggio's Italian Deli, 54
Star Market & Catering, 44
Staropolska Deli, 62
Tedi's Polish Deli, 63
Tony's Italian Sausage, 54
Valente's Deli Bakery, 55
Zaidy's Deli, 59

PASTA PLACES

Pasta Pasta Pasta, 64

SPECIALTY MEAT & FISH

Cherry Crest Market, 65
Dale's Exotic Game Meats, 66
Fred's Fine Meats, 66
Herb's Meats, 66
Louisiana/Texas Catfish, 67
Oliver's Meat Market, 68
Sam's Meat Market, 68
Sir Loin Meat Shoppe, 68
Uncle Milt's Fine Meats, 69
Wally's Quality Meats, 69

CHEESE SHOPS

The Cheese Company, 70

MARKETS

Air–Afrik, 71
Aladdin, 108

Alfalfa's Markets, 117
Arash Supermarket, 107
Aromas Market, 118
Asian Deli, 72
Asian Market, 72
Aurora Asian Market, 73
Big T Market, 116
Black Forest Specialties, 92
Bombay Bazaar, 93
Canos Collection, 88
Chili Store, 101
Compleat Gourmet & Gifts, 128
Cook's Mart, 129
Cosolo's Italian Market, 97
Creative Cook, 129
Damavand Market, 110
Denver Buffalo Company, 118
Denver Oriental
 Supermarket, 74
Economy Greek Market, 111
El Azteca Grocery, 102
English Teacup, 88
European Mart, Inc., 115
Garramone's Farm Market, 120
Garramone's Fruits &
 Vegetables, 121
Greens Market, 121
Gourmet Foods Warehouse, 122
House of Windsor, 89
Indochina Enterprises, 74
International Market, 112
Johnny's Grocery
 & Market, 103
Krungthai Market, 76
La Popular Tortillas
 & Tamales, 104
Laotian Oriental Food Store, 76
Lek's Asian Market, 77
Lemon Cheese Company, 90
Little Saigon Supermarket, 78
Market, The, 124
Mekong, 79
Middle East Market, 113
Midopa Market, 79
Morocco International Food
 Market, 114

Nipa Hut, 91
Old San Juan Groceries, 106
Old Santa Fe Pottery, 123
Oriental Grocery Market,
Oriental Food Market, 81
Oriental Grocery Store, 82
Oriental Market, 82
Pacific Mercantile, 83
Pacific Ocean Marketplace, 84
Pete's Fruits & Vegetables, 124
Romano's Gourmet Market, 125
Seoul Oriental Market, 84
Spinelli's, 98
Tajmahal Imports, 95
Tan Phat Oriental Market, 85
Tejal International Foods, 95
The Market, 124
Tony's Meats & Specialty
 Foods, 126
Utica Grocery, 100
Vinnola's Italian Market, 98
Wild Oats Market, 127
Xuan Trang, 87

GOURMET COOKWARE

Compleat Gourmet, 128
Cook's Mart, 129
Creative Cook, 129
Kitchen Nouveau, 130
Peppercorn, 131
Williams-Sonoma, 131

ICE CREAM

All for the Better, 140
Bonnie Brae Ice Cream, 141
Boulder Ice Cream, 141
Ice Cream Makers, 141
Josh & John's, 142
Liks, 142
Magill's World of Ice Cream, 142
Soda Rock Fountain, 143

CHOCOLATE

Blume's Chocolates, 133
Chocolate Foundry, 133
Cocolo, 134
Dietrich's Chocolate & Espresso, 134
Divine Temptations, 136
Enstrom Candies, 136
Godiva Chocolatier, 136-7
Hammond Candy Co., 137
Lydia's Inc., 137
Rocky Mountain Chocolate Factory, 138
Russell Stover Candies, 138
See's Candies, 138-9
Stephany's Chocolates, 139
Sweet Expressions 139

COFFEE SHOPS

Bookend Cafe, 144
Boyer Coffee Company, 145
Caffée Arabica, 145
Colorado Espresso, 146
Common Grounds, 146
Java Creek, 147
Java Hut, 147
Jitters Internet Cafe, 148
Latta's Espresso Company, 148
Market, 149
Neighborhood Buzz, 149
Old World Tea & Coffee, 149
Paris on the Platte, 150
Peaberry Coffee Ltd., 150
Penny Lane, 151
St. Mark's Coffee House, 151
Starbucks Coffee Company, 152
Terra of the Earth, 152
The Market, 149
Trident Booksellers, 153

RECIPE INDEX

Aigo bouido, 123
Apricot chicken, 113
Arroz verde con guajillo, 102
Ceviche, 104
Chana bhatura, 96
Chicken a l'orientale, 128
Chinese garlic custard, 87
Christmas stollen, 31
Couscous salad, 114
Dumplings w/red oil sauce, 75
Garlic pizza crust, 35
Glace, 92
Goi cuon, 81
Greek roasted chicken, 111
Italian barbeque sauce, 97
Masaman curry, 86
Milanesa, 106

Moe's appetizer, 70
Nuoc cham, 81
Old-fashioned coffee soda, 151
Pesto a la Victoria, 50
Polenta, 56
Posole, 61
Quick guacamole, 107
Quitheo, 119
Rosehip marmalade, 130
Sam's teriyaki sauce, 67
Seafood pizza, 122
Shrimp amartriciana, 99
Shrimp creole, 126
Smoked salmon appetizer, 127
Spaghetti con olio e aglio, 65
Stuffed cabbage leaves, 63
Trifle, 27

Ethnic Adventures...

If you're interested in being on our mailing list for tours of ethnic markets, and any other events we may take it into our heads to plan, such as cooking classes, ethnic dinners, or an ethnic newsletter, please send us your name, address and phone number and tell us what your interestes are. We'll do our best to accommodate you.

>Better Business Communications
>957 S. Cole Drive
>Lakewood, CO 80228

ORDERING MORE BOOKS

If you'd like to order more books, or to order copies of our other book, **More Adventures in Eating: Denver's Ethnic Restaurants**, please send your name, address and phone number, together with a check for $13 for each book, to cover sales tax, shipping and handling. Send to

>Better Business Communications
>957 S. Cole Drive
>Lakewood, CO 80228

Please specify which book(s) you want. Make checks payable to Better Business Communications

Quantity discounts available